The
JOURNEY
BEYOND
LIFE VOLUME
ONE

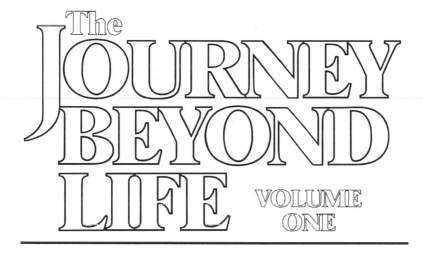

The JOURNEY BEYOND LIFE

VOLUME ONE

MICHELE R. SORENSEN
DR. DAVID R. WILLMORE

Sounds of Zion

First printing August 1988
Second printing December 1988
Third printing September 1989
Fourth printing October 1990
Fifth printing January 1992
Sixth printing November 1993

Library of Congress Cataloging-in-Publication Data

Sorensen, Michele R., 1962 -
Willmore, David R., 1938 -
    The Journey Beyond Life

        Includes index and bibliography.
        1. Spirit life beyond death--Mormon authors.
        ISBN 0-910613-15-X 1988 I. Title. 88-81163

Contents

Acknowledgments

Prologue   i

SECTION I: Death

  1   The Journey From Here To There   3

SECTION II: Contact With Spirits

  2   Family Concern   33
  3   Involvement   59

SECTION III: Spirit World Environment

  4   Preliminary Judgment   87
  5   A Beautiful World   104
  6   The Return   129

SECTION IV: Spirit World Activities

  7   Missionary Work   145
  8   Genealogical and Temple Work   165
  9   Progression Towards Perfection   190

Epilogue   206

Bibliography   219

Index   225

Acknowledgments

We express our deepest gratitude to our families and friends who have provided so much support and encouragement. Appreciation is also extended to those who have shared personal experiences for the growth and betterment of others. We respect the request of many of those contributors who wish to remain anonymous due to the sacred nature of their journey and experiences beyond the veil.

Prologue

Skiing accidents ruined both my knees. First, I tore the ligaments in my right knee as I was trying to help a fallen skier. Then, eleven months later, I tried to ski again and fell, ruining my left knee. I had surgery immediately, but there were painful complications that at times threatened to pull down my health as well as my spirits during my freshman year at BYU.

One afternoon, as I sat in a child development class, watching big, wet snowflakes glide down as if someone had broken open a feather pillow, I began to grow inexplicably weary. My eyes began to burn and water, and I could hardly hold my head up. All I could think of was the snowflakes as the teacher's voice droned farther and farther away.

The bell rang, and my roommate Ann came to meet me, cheerful as always. "You look awful," she said. From Ann, such a comment was perfectly acceptable and even funny.

I got up and began "crutching" across campus toward my next class. But when I came to the building, Ann made it clear that she was not letting me go in.

"I'm serious," she said. "Come home and rest. You don't look like you could even sit up."

I had never skipped a single class since coming to BYU, but I followed her like a child, without willpower to think it through myself. I had an intense desire to leave the wet sidewalk and lie down where the snow was blanketing the

grass. And maybe, just maybe, I would lie there
forever and catch one or two snowflakes on my
tongue. I was unbearably hot.

Back in our apartment, I put on a nightgown
and lay down. The next thing I remember was
Ann and Carrie deciding that my fever was too
high. Somehow they moved me into the living
room and I lay on our ugly red and green plaid
couch. My fever continued to rise, but all I could
do was stare through water eyes at the snowflakes
falling outside. When my temperature topped
105°, I remember hearing Carrie and Ann decide
to wet a sheet with cold water and drape it over
me. I was already suffering a great deal of pain
from the chills that were racking my injured leg.
Inwardly I cringed at the thought of the cold
sheet, but I didn't have the strength to argue. The
shock from the sheet was terrible, and it did
nothing to my fever.

My roommates talked about calling the
hospital while I stared out the window. Irrational
in my pain, I started thinking that I would rather
die than go back to the hospital. I began to say
over and over in my mind, "I will die before I'll
go back to the hospital." As I watched the peaceful
snowflakes, I heard Carrie and Ann say my fever
was still climbing. I'm not sure why they never
called a nurse. Ann went somewhere to talk to
someone, and Carrie sat at the table studying,
only a few feet away from me.

I couldn't tell if I was delirious, or dreaming,
or if something else had happened, but suddenly
I was above my body, looking down from the
corner above the window. My leg didn't hurt a
bit. Nothing hurt. My body looked awful there, so
white and uncomfortable. I was warm now, but

my eyes were not burning. I felt a wonderful, golden warmth with no painful chills. Someone was standing behind me. The warmth seemed to come from that person and spread around me, like a pair of arms. I didn't turn around; I just stared with relief at the form on that ugly couch. Nor was I the least bit tired. I was at peace — I knew I was dead. Then I thought, "I should have done this sooner!" Realization spread immediately over me that my faith in the plan of salvation was valid. This was proof.

In the years since, I have had a hard time understanding how the person spoke to me. I have felt like I was putting words into his mouth. Yet, he communicated to me, and the communication was so loving and so peaceful, that I know the warmth and beautiful golden-white light that was around me came from his love. He knew what I had been through, and his understanding and compassion put me at complete ease. Only recently have I realized it was telepathic communication, and that is why I couldn't find words to equal what was said or the love that was with it. Thoughts were clearly communicated into my mind. Putting it in words, our exchange went something like this:

"You're dead, you know."

"I know. It's great."

"Do you truly want to be dead?"

"Oh yes! Why not? This is all so wonderful." I thought of the relief, the light, the love.

Then I saw Ann come around the corner and put her hand to my body's forehead. She screamed and tried to find a pulse. It was all so far away, but so clear. The sound of her scream didn't jar me a bit, but the way she was upset was very

very immediate to me. Carrie grabbed the phone, but couldn't seem to think of a number. They were saying, "She's dead, she's dead." Katherine, another roommate, came in and saw me. She pointed my folks' number out to Carrie on the paper by the phone.

I thought, "It's all right. They will get over it. We are just roommates, and I couldn't have meant all that much to them. They'll be better off not having to help me around and put up with my crutches and my struggles."

No reply, just love.

I saw my mother's face where the phone was. I saw my whole family. They called my brother overseas. An entire network of phone lines with people on the other end spread before my view. I was surprised to find that I felt every emotion they experienced, but my euphoria overshadowed my empathy.

"Yes, I was pretty selfish not to think of how my family was going to feel. Still, all those people will get over it. They are just surprised. But really, this is the most natural thing. I feel like I belong here. They will all get over it. Even my mother and father and brothers and sister. They didn't want me to be going through such pain. If they could have known what it was like they would know I'm better off this way. They are strong in the gospel and people always go on after a death. It will pass. We'll be together again." I probably didn't sound as calm as I was trying to feel. Yet the voice behind me was the same as before.

"But look what you're missing."

I saw a blonde man walking up to the temple. I didn't know who he was, but I knew somehow that he was a fantastic person, and I really felt like I was missing out. Although I only saw him from behind, I could tell he had on a suit. He had a boy with fair skin and hair by one hand and a girl by the other. They were little, beautiful children, excited about seeing the temple. The little girl jumped up and down and her ruffly skirt and strawberry-blonde curls bounced. I knew this was symbolic, a promise of motherhood and of being married to this man for eternity. It seemed at that moment that nothing in the world or out of it could be more desirable. Being a mother and a wife was the whole reason for existence. The warmth was still around me, but the vestiges of the bliss I had felt were suddenly temporary, as I began to waver about the joys of being dead, at least before experiencing the fullness of life.

"The choice is yours."

I was thinking, feeling. I was gazing again at that still body that looked so relieved from hurt.

"Yes," I said fervently. I want to go back."

"It is not going to be easy. There will be pain and sorrow."

"I want to go back."

And I did.

I was shaking fiercely and my leg ached inside and trembled with goosebumps and chills. Before I opened my eyes I started crying, "I was dead! I was dead!"

Carrie ran over from where she had been sitting at the table studying. What I had seen must have been a foreshadowing, since no one had yet noticed there was anything unusual about me.

"You're delirious or something," she said, taking my hand. "It's all right. Relax."

Ann came in the room. "That's it. I'm calling the hospital."

"No." I calmed down suddenly at that. "No. I'll be fine. Just get someone in here to give me a blessing. That is what I need." She went straight out the door, and I closed my eyes and waited.

I guess Ann asked the first two men she could find in the lounge. I didn't know them, but they gave me a blessing that I would rest well, and they promised me that Heavenly Father had a certain priesthood holder in mind for me, and that when the time came to be married, I would know. I slept after that and awoke in the evening, feeling better than I had felt for days.

I received the same blessing about the "certain priesthood holder" three more times in the next two years by priesthood holders who did not know each other. I also had the same promise made to me one other time in a moment of inspiration by a General Authority. I have since married a fine, and incidentally, blonde priesthood holder in the temple whom I knew was the one the blessings had indicated.

I eventually had to have another operation on my leg, because a staph infection was in the marrow, but with time I healed.

This experience changed my life. At times when things are difficult, I am impressed, almost as if being reminded, that I chose to be here and I welcomed whatever would come my way — even the sorrow, because it is necessary to have joy. I have no fear of death, but only of not accomplishing all that I need to do in this life.

In this special experience, the veil that lies over mortality was parted in order to kindle within one young woman a spark of enlightened perspective and guidance, so that she would not lose sight of her priorities and make a choice she might forever regret. Yet, in spite of this indication of her worth in the sight of heaven, can we conclude that the rest of her life has been simple and that she has no further need for faith? Hardly. That is not the purpose of our mortal existence.

In the 16th chapter of Luke in the Bible, Jesus taught a parable about the beggar Lazarus and a rich man who died at nearly the same time. The rich man realized certain things once he was on the other side of the veil, and the reality of this knowledge moved him to plead with Abraham that Lazarus be sent back to preach repentance to his (the rich man's) family. Abraham replies,

"They have Moses and the prophets; let them hear them."

"Nay, Father Abraham; but if one went unto them from the dead, they will repent," the rich man says.

But Abraham patiently replies, "If they hear not Moses and the prophets, neither will they be persuaded though one rose from the dead."

Does the Lord fling aside the veil and let knowledge pour through unrestrained and indefinitely? Are we spiritually prepared enough for it? It seems more likely that we must discover pearls of knowledge, uncovering them gently, with the care born of having paid a great price for such a treasure. Does God bury knowledge behind impenetrable locks that have no keys? Perhaps, instead, He shrouds some knowledge behind a veil, lest we take it for granted. Then, from time to time, He parts the veil and allows us to learn bit by bit about Him and His creations. Through the learning and discovering process we become prepared to receive more and more knowledge.

We call this further knowledge the "mysteries" and we rightly hesitate to delve too deeply or dwell too heavily on it. The things which God openly reveals are vital to our testimonies, and it is on these truths that we should base our faith. However, seeking further knowledge is not an unrighteous desire. Concerning the next life and the workings of the eternities, the Prophet Joseph Smith has said:

> . . .it is but reasonable to suppose that God would reveal something in reference to the matter, and it is a subject we ought to study more than any other. . .If we have any claim on our Heavenly Father for anything, it is for knowledge on this important subject.[1]

So, we should seek for greater understanding, and when we do so, praying with fervent sincerity, we fill find that our agency brushes up against the unending wisdom and love of our Heavenly Father. We sense that there are vast realms beyond what we know, and our petitions, though important to us, seem trivial. In these moments, when we feel so close to our Eternal Father and yet separate, the veil hangs between us almost like a tangible reality.

---

[1] Joseph Smith, *History of the Church,* 2nd ed., Salt Lake City, UT: Deseret Book Co., 1959, Vol. VI, p. 50.

Each of us has at some time sensed the veil. When a baby is born we feel the veil's sweeping pass with awe. And when we sit beside the bed of a dying loved one, watching him bid farewell to all that is so familiar, we can feel the reality of his new birth and the joy of reunion with those who have waited for him beyond. In those moments when the veil is so real to us that we almost feel it has touched our cheek as it stretches over one we love, we realize that we have been taught more than we can say. We feel a nearness to our Father, a peaceful serenity that is too deep for words.

There are times when death is surrounded by trauma, and those who lose a loved one are too harried by the extremity of the situation to sense the lingering touch and the promise of the veil.

For these individuals' distress, and with an eye to the future that each of us must face, we have gathered a collection of experiences from interviews, unpublished manuscripts, and published works that shed light on the world beyond. Naturally, the accounts differ in particulars because of the individuality in expression and perceptions of those who relate them. In most cases we have shared the first name of the individual, but some people preferred to remain entirely anonymous and we have respected their wishes. People are generally reluctant to talk openly about such experiences, because they hold them sacred, and they struggle to find a way to express things our language has no words to communicate. However, when we consider enough of these experiences, we can form impressions of what lies beyond the veil that will strengthen our love for our Savior, erase our fear of death in the reality of the other side, and motivate us to live better lives. It seems that in nearly every brush with death, we learn a little more about our eternal selves, and we feel more clearly the significance of our family relationships.

In the chapters to come, then, we will present some of what is known about the realm beyond mortality. Our overall intent is one of spiritual upliftment and not clinical accuracy.

Yet we urge you to note that there are many types of revelation, i.e., visions, dreams, near death, and out-of-the-body experiences. Each experience shared here will make mention of its type, and we urge you to weigh it accordingly. Each set of stories are followed by commonly asked questions about spirits and the spirit world. Through careful research we have provided some answers.

SECTION I

Death

1

The Journey From Here To There

The nicest feeling came over me. I had the peaceful feeling you get when you receive a testimony. Then my mother suddenly jumped up and ran from the room. The next thing I remember was being three or four feet above the bed. Doctors and nurses were working on my body, working and working on it. But I did not want to go back. I struggled — I really fought — against returning. Being there was the most wonderful feeling I have ever experienced in my entire life.

I was a twenty-four-year-old university student, engaged to be married soon. I had gone home over Christmas break for a hernia repair at the old Mount Pleasant Hospital. I was in the recovery room phasing in and out when I suddenly found myself above them, looking down. I wasn't floating; I was just up above. I could see my body very clearly, and I could see what they were doing to it.

The next thing I remember was my mother waking me up. Two or three hours had passed since the time I had gone out. Neither my mother nor the doctors would ever tell me what happened. I'm sure they were afraid to tell me they had lost me. I didn't share this experience with anyone for three or four years, and since that time I have only told three people. To me, the whole thing is something very, very special. Once, several years later, I spoke to my mother about what had happened, and she admitted that as she sat there she saw my body fall, just collapse on the pillow. That was when she ran out and got the doctor and came back.

I can still see it all so clearly, especially the doctors and nurses working on me, picking up my feet and elevating them. I saw them putting tubes in me and sticking me. What they were doing was very clear then and is still vivid in my memory. I know there is a difference between the body and the spirit. I saw my body, yet I was not there.

That's all I remember — looking back down and seeing my body below me, with them working on it. I remember best the feeling of real peace. I did *not* want to go back.

A remarkable thing happened to Richard during that Christmas break when he went home for surgery — he died. Encounters with death are powerful, life-changing occurrences. Although each experience is as unique as the individual who has it, comparing more than one account reveals some consistent features and the death experience takes shape:

In the spring of 1980, I was the president of a young company, as well as the director of several other firms. On top of this, I was a counselor in my ward's bishopric and a father of five. I had been feeling a lot of stress and tightness in my chest, but I continued to shrug it off and keep working.

One Friday night, everyone had gone home from work except my general manager, my brother, and me. They had started to leave and I was at my desk cleaning things up when I began to feel uneasy. My chest grew tight as I got up and headed for the door — then everything went blank. My balance was gone and I felt myself falling. I called out, hoping someone was still there. But my voice was far away, echoing as I fell. My chest felt like it was being crushed tighter and tighter in a vise, until suddenly the pressure was gone. All at once I began floating upward. I must have been almost to the ceiling before I stopped. Everything was peaceful.

All around me was a bright light, especially above the ceiling; yet I turned and looked down at the scene below. From my position, I saw my body on the floor with my general manager and brother bent over it. I was enjoying the peaceful feeling so much that the only desire I had was to remain where I was.

Soon, however, I intensely wanted to go farther into the light. Since I could feel no pain at all, going back didn't even occur to me. For fifteen years I had suffered from chronic back pain, but now, being in this spirit state with no pain was very enjoyable. Normally I can't see three feet without my glasses, yet I could see everything perfectly. Though I was capable of viewing miles around me, all I looked at when I turned from the light was the two men bent over my body. And that was why I didn't go on.

The next thing I remember was the tightness coming into my chest again. I could feel that there were a lot of people around me, and opening my eyes, I could faintly see their hats and the blue of their uniforms. I could hear them talking, but their words were unclear and distant like an echo. Tubes were in my nose and arms and people were pushing on my chest. All the time I tried to force myself away. I wanted to go back.

Later, in the hospital, I learned that I had experienced a stress attack, not a heart attack, but something very close to one. My friends had heard me calling someone's name, and then my pulse was gone.

My brother phoned the paramedics, while my general manager administered to me until my brother came over and joined him. The paramedics arrived within seven minutes. I still had no pulse, but they were able to resuscitate me and get me to the hospital.

The whole experience aged me about ninety years. Thirty-three is pretty young to have that type of problem, so I began to take life a lot easier. My wife and I have seven children now, and I make it a point to spend more time with my family. The gospel also means more in my life. My commitment to it and to living this life better are far greater than ever before. The experience was priceless, and because of its sacred nature, I haven't related it to anyone other than my family and close personal friends.

I'll tell you what I would do if this happened to me again: I would stay. Being there, out of my body and this world, was much more peaceful and enjoyable than being here. Of course, I knew then that I could not go any further: it wasn't my time. It was as if there was a block or something. The priesthood blessing, their praying, made the difference. But next time, if I had a choice...

These two experiences illustrate what an out-of-body encounter with death is like. Although we usually hear accounts of death from the viewpoint of those who have sat with a dying friend or relative, even second-person accounts reveal the same consistent features that are found in first-hand accounts.

When Leon died, his family stayed near his bedside, as recorded in this account:

Dad died in 1983 in the Gunnison Hospital. Although he had been sick for a long time, he was very coherent between his bouts with a high fever. We would think he was recovering, but then the fever would return. It was plain that he was trying to die. Over and over he would say, "Pull me through! Pull me through!"

One day he was talking to his own dad, his mother, and his granddad, all of whom had been dead for many years. He kept asking them to pull him through. That night when I went to the hospital to be with him, he sat up and talked to me as clearly as you and I are talking.

"Richard, can't you pull me through? Can't you get me through it? I've got to get through that."

"Pull you through what?"

"Oh, you don't understand," he said, but he kept wanting somebody to pull him through something.

Whenever he talked to the people who were dead, it seemed very clear that they were on the other side of a tunnel, a hole, or a tube. He made it plain that he had to get through something to be where his parents were. He continued pleading to be pulled through until he finally passed away.

In a near death experience, someone dies but is resuscitated. Both near death and second-person descriptions (such as this one of Leon's passing), reveal a pattern of common elements. The next section looks at these consistent features as well as some frequently asked questions about dying and near death experiences. The answers draw briefly on scriptural, authoritative, and literary sources, as well as personal accounts.

Questions and Answers

1. What is death?

Since the beginning of time, inspired men and women have attempted to explain the meaning of death and what lies beyond mortality:

> Life is eternal; and love is immortal; and death is only a horizon; and a horizon is nothing save the limit of our sight.[1]

> This world is the land of the dying; the next is the land of the living.[2]

Elder Boyd K. Packer of the Quorum of Twelve Apostles has said, "It is important that you get in your mind what death is. Death is a separation."[3] In considering this, if we think about the death of the Savior on the cross, we will remember that He cried with a loud voice, "Father, into thy hands I commend my spirit: and, having said thus, he gave up the ghost" (Luke 23:46). Clearly, His spirit left His body, and this separation is what we call "death."

---

[1] Rossiter Worthington Raymond as quoted by Richard L. Evans in *Richard Evans' Quote Book*, Salt Lake City, Ut.: Publisher's Press, 1971, p. 115.

[2] Tyron Edwards as quoted by Alma P. and Clea M. Burton, *For They Shall Be Comforted*. Salt Lake City, Ut.: Deseret Book Co., 1964, p. 51.

[3] Boyd K. Packer, *That All May Be Edified*. Salt Lake City, Ut.: Bookcraft, Inc., 1982, p. 17.

Robert Blatchford wrote a book entitled *God and My Neighbor,* in which he vigorously attacked many accepted Christian beliefs including God, Christ, and immortality. He was certain that there was no room for anyone to challenge his watertight arguments, until one day when something happened that left him groping his way back to the faith he had worked so hard to denounce. What shattered the wisdom he thought he possessed? His wife died. After looking with a broken heart on her mortal remains, he realized that the only thing missing was something intangible — her soul. Blatchford wrote:

> Death is not what some people imagine. It is only like going into another room. In that other room we shall find...the dear women and men and the sweet children we have loved and lost.[4]

Considering Robert Blatchford's experience and countless others, a meaningful explanation of death is that it is a journey of the spirit from the mortal world to the spirit world. Regarding this journey, Elder Sterling W. Sill explained:

> ...the most important event in life is death. We live to die and then we die to live. Death is a kind of graduation day for life. It is our only means of entrance to our eternal lives. And it seems to me to be a very helpful procedure to spend a little time pre-living our death. That is,

---

[4]Thomas S. Monson, *The Ensign,* April 1982, p. 9.

what kind of person would you like to be when the last hour of your life arrives?[5]

No matter how carefully we study death, it is most likely that we will eventually conclude, as did the apostle Paul:[6]

> For now we see through a glass, darkly; but then face to face: now I know in part; but then shall I know even as also I am known. (I Corinthians 13:12)

2. *In what ways are birth and death alike? How do they differ?*

There are some remarkable similarities between birth and death. Elder Bruce R. McConkie said:

> We know that this great plan of progression called for a *birth* which would provide a mortal tabernacle for our eternal spirits, and for a *death* which would free those spirits from the frailties, diseases, and weaknesses of mortality.[7]

The words birth and death both describe movement. Birth describes our movement from the spirit world to mortality. Death describes our movement from mortality to the spirit world. With each movement we terminate our existence in one place and initiate our existence in another.

---

[5]Sterling W. Sill, Conference Report, October 1976.

[6]For further reference, see question #1 in Chapter 6.

[7]Bruce R. McConkie, in Conference Report, (Oct. 1976), p. 157-159. (Italics added)

When God sends forth a tiny soul
To learn the ways of earth,
A mother's love is waiting here —
We call this wonder — birth.

When God calls home a tired soul
And stills a fleeting breath,
A Father's love is waiting there
This too is birth — not death.
                              Author Unknown

3. Are there "near death" or "out-of-the-body" experiences recorded in the scriptures?

The scriptures contain several accounts of people who have been brought back from the dead. Elijah raised the son of the widow of Zarephath and Elisha raised the son of the Shunamite woman. Jesus raised the son of the widow of Nain, the daughter of Jairus, and Lazarus of Bethany. However, none of these cases record information about what happened while these individuals' spirits were absent from their bodies.

Two New Testament accounts where information was shared from beyond the veil are the stoning of Stephen and a special vision given to the Apostle Paul:

When they heard these things, they were cut to the heart, and they gnashed on him with their teeth. But he, being full of the Holy Ghost, looked up stedfastly into heaven, and saw the glory of God, and Jesus standing on the right hand of God, And said, Behold, I see the heavens opened, the Son of man standing on the right hand of God. (Acts 7:54-56)

I knew a man in Christ above fourteen years ago, (whether in the body, I cannot tell; or whether out of the body, I cannot tell: God knoweth;) such an one caught up to the third heaven...How that he was caught up into paradise, and heard unspeakable words, which it is not lawful for a man to utter (II Cor. 12:2,4).

Although many prophets since the fall of Adam have received marvelous visions concerning the heavens and what lies beyond the veil, it has not been until the restoration of the Gospel, that information gained from near death or out-of-the-body experiences has become more accessible.

4. *What do people experience when they die? Is it painful or pleasant?*

We sometimes congratulate ourselves at the moment of waking from a troubled dream: it may be so the moment after death.[8]

Hugh B. Brown said:

I wonder whether we are now preparing — in this figuratively speaking pre-natal life — to be born into the new and more glorious world.

---

[8]Nathaniel Hawthorne as quoted by Richard L. Evans, *Richard Evans' Quote Book*, p. 116.

When we are born into that life, I think we shall
find God has prepared us for that birth.[9]

Brigham Young suggested:

Probably, in most cases, the change from
mortality to immortality is no greater, comparatively speaking, than when a child emerges into
this world. We shall suffer no more in putting off
this flesh and leaving the spirit houseless than
the child, in its capacity, does in its first efforts to
breathe the breath of this mortal life.[10]

Others have written vivid descriptions of near
death or out-of-the-body experiences that they have
had, and these accounts are astoundingly similar to
the first-hand experiences related earlier in this
chapter. For example, on 3 March, 1891, Ella Jensen,
a fifteen-year-old Sunday School teacher, described
her experience in the spirit world after being absent
from her body for three and a half hours. She said:

I could see people from the other world and
hear the most delightful music and singing that I
had ever heard. This singing lasted for six hours,
during which time I was preparing to leave this
earth, and I could hear it (the music) all through
the house. At ten o'clock my spirit left my body. It
took me some time to make up my mind to go,
as I could see and hear the folks crying over me.
Although it was hard for me to leave them, as

---

[9] Burton, *For They Shall Be Comforted*, p. 45-47.

[10] Burton, *For They Shall Be Comforted*, p. 57.

soon as I had a glimpse of the other world, I was anxious to go and all care and worry left me.

...there was practically no pain on leaving the body in death, but the intense pain was almost unbearable in coming back to life.[11]

Peter E. Johnson made a journey to the spirit world while serving a mission in September of 1898. He described it this way:

My spirit left the body; just how I cannot tell. But I perceived myself standing some four or five feet in the air and saw my body lying on the bed. I felt perfectly natural, but this was a new condition. I began to make observations. I turned my head, shrugged my shoulders, felt with my hands, and realized that it was myself. I also knew that my body was lying, lifeless on the bed.[12]

Walter P. Monson wrote of his experience:

At midnight I was fully awake. I heard Christmas chimes and felt the nurse taking my pulse and temperature. Suddenly, a coldness attacked my feet and hands, moving up my limbs and up my arms toward my body. I felt it reach my heart. There was a slight murmur. I gasped for breath and lapsed into unconsciousness, so far as all things mortal.

---

[11]Gordon T. Allred, *If A Man Die*, Salt Lake City, Ut.: Bookcraft, Inc., 1964, pp. 120-121.

[12]Peter E. Johnson, "A Testimony," *The Relief Society Magazine*, Vol. VII, No. 8, Aug. 1920.

...then I awoke in full possession of all faculties in another sphere of life. I stood apart from my body and looked at it. I noticed that its eyes were partly closed and that the chin had dropped. I was now without pain, and the joy and freedom I felt and the peace of mind that came over me were the sweetest sensations I had ever experienced. I lost all sense of time and space. The law of gravitation had no hold on me.[13]

Individual elements and the general feeling of these experiences are usually repeated in near death or out-of-the-body situations.

Information gained through scientific research:

5. *What scientific evidence is there to support the first-hand experiences cited in this chapter?*

One important source is the work of Dr. Raymond Moody. In one glance at his writings, we can see that basic elements are remarkably the same. Consider the similarities between the preceding accounts and his description of the experience of dying. He writes.

Despite the wide variation in the circumstances surrounding close calls with death and in the types of persons undergoing them, it remains true that there is a striking similarity among the accounts of the experiences themselves. In fact,

---

[13]Dorothy South Hackworth, (comp) *The Master's Touch*, Salt Lake City, Ut.: Bookcraft Inc., 1961, p. 60.

the similarities among various reports are so
great that one can easily pick out about fifteen
separate elements which recur again and again in
the mass of narratives that I have collected. On
the basis of these points of likeness, let me now
construct a brief theoretically "ideal" or
"complete" experience which embodies all of the
common elements, in the order which it is typi-
cal for them to occur:

'A man is dying and, as he reaches the point
of greatest physical distress, he *hears himself pronounced dead* by his doctor. He begins to *hear an
uncomfortable noise*, loud ringing or buzzing,
and at the same time feels himself *moving very
rapidly through a long dark tunnel*. After this, he
suddenly finds himself *outside of his own physical body* but still in the immediate physical environment, and he sees his own body from a distance, as though he is a spectator. He watches the
resuscitation attempt from this unusual vantage
point and is in a state of emotional upheaval...
'After a while, he collects himself and be-
comes more accustomed to his odd condition. He
notices that he still has a "body," but one of a very
different nature and with very different powers
from the physical body he has left behind...'[14]

Dr. Moody further discusses each of the common elements in his model of the death experience, and cautions the reader to keep in mind that
the model is not meant to be a representation of

---

[14]Raymond Moody, Jr., M.D., *Life After Life*, St. Simons Island, Ga.:
Mockingbird Books, 1975, p. 21.

any single experience, but a composite of common elements included in many accounts.[15] The first six elements are:

1. Ineffability: inexpressible, defies description
2. Hearing the News
3. Feelings of Peace and Quiet
4. The Noise
5. The Dark Tunnel
6. Out of the Body

In comparing Dr. Moody's outline with the experiences we have collected, we have found that all of them are duplicated except the uncomfortable noise. The only mention of "noise" in our research is in connection with music or singing that was heard by the dying individual.

Dr. Elizabeth Kuebler-Ross, a Chicago doctor who has studied hundreds of patients that died and were revived moments later through medical resuscitation, reports similar circumstances. These patients had reached a point where there were no vital signs or brain waves. Upon death, they perceived an immediate separation of a spirit-like self from their bodies. This spirit then became aware of its former body still lying in bed. The patients reported great feelings of peace and ease:

> If people were in the room trying to revive their bodies, the 'dead persons' tried hard to communicate that everything was all right, that

---

[15] Altogether Dr. Moody detailed fifteen elements, and he later added four more in his sequel, *Reflections on Life After Life*.

death wasn't that bad. Finding it impossible to communicate with either family or medical personnel in the room, the spirit then turns its attention upwards.[16]

6. *Since it is common for people to fear death, what can help them deal with it?*

People fear death for many reasons. Among these are that it terminates relationships between people, it is nearly always accompanied by emotional upheaval or trauma, any promise of a life beyond is unconfirmed by the senses, and many lack hope or faith in life after death.

In spite of this inspired men and women throughout history have written to dispel fear and provide hope for each of us who must die one day. Socrates said: "Be of good cheer about death, and know this as a truth, that no evil can happen to a good man, either in life or after death."[17]

The greatest source of comfort and helpful reassurance is contained in the scriptures. The Savior said:

> . . . I am the resurrection, and the life: he that believeth in me, though he were dead, yet shall he live:
> And whosoever liveth and believeth in me shall never die. (John 11:25-26)

---

[16] Bill Mandell, "Study Shows Death Placid Experience," *Knight Newspapers*, Philadelphia. See also Elizabeth Kuebler-Ross, *On Death and Dying*, New York: MacMillan, 1969.

[17] Burton, *For They Shall Be Comforted*, p. 49.

For God so loved the world, that he gave his only begotten Son, that whosoever believeth in him should not perish, but have everlasting life. (John 3:16)

Peace I leave with you, my peace I give unto you: not as the world giveth, give I unto you. Let not your heart be troubled, neither let it be afraid. (John 14:27).

In our our time, there has been much written to provide comfort and understanding of the death experience. President David O. McKay said:

There is no cause to fear death; it is but an incident in life. It is as natural as birth. Why should we fear it? Some fear it because they think it is the end of life, and life often is the dearest thing we have. Eternal life is man's greatest blessing. If only man would "do His will" instead of looking hopelessly at the dark and gloomy tomb, they would turn their eyes heavenward and know that "Christ is risen!" With all my soul I know that death is conquered by Jesus Christ.[18]

The most important thing for each of us to remember as we approach anyone's death, is to acquire a testimony which will provide some insulation for us against the separation and trauma we must face when death occurs. With such armor, the fear of death is diminished, and we are not inclined to grieve endlessly over the loss of loved ones. Then each of us may be able to approach death as

---

[18]Burton, *For They Shall Be Comforted*, p. 45.

Elder Bruce R. McConkie did when, one month prior to his own passing, he said:

> I am one of his witnesses, and in a coming day I shall feel the nail marks in his hands and in his feet and shall wet his feet with my tears.
> But I shall not know any better then than I know now that he is God's almighty son, that he is our Savior, and Redeemer, and that salvation comes in and through his atoning blood and in no other way."[19]

7. *What is meant by the scriptural phrase "And Their Death Shall be Sweet?"*

This phrase comes from the Doctrine and Covenants, Section 42, verses 46-47:.

> And it shall come to pass that those that die in me shall not taste of death, for it shall be sweet unto them; And they that die not in me, wo unto them, for their death is bitter.

In Revelation 14:13, we find a similar verse:

> . . . Blessed are the dead which die in the Lord from henceforth: Yea, saith the Spirit, that they may rest from their labours; and their works do follow them.

To die 'in me' or to die 'in the Lord' does not suggest that we be perfect in this life: Jesus was the only perfect man. However, we must be seeking

---

[19]Bruce R. McConkie, in Conference Report, (Apr. 1985), p. 12.

perfection through Christ, living His gospel —
keeping His commandments, having a testimony
of His life and His mission. Then we no longer fear
death and when we die, we are secure. We will
know the following inspired statement is true:

> For as in Adam *all* die, even so in Christ shall
> *all* be made alive. (I Cor. 15:22) (Italics added.)

Men from all ages have believed in the immortality of the soul. For them, death would undoubt-
edly be more sweet or pleasant than for the unbe-
liever or the skeptic. The well-known playwright
Thornton Wilder put it this way:

> I don't care what they say with their mouths
> — everybody knows that something is eternal.
> And it ain't houses, and it ain't names, and it
> ain't earth, and it ain't even the stars — every-
> body knows in their bones that something is
> eternal, and that something has to do with hu-
> man beings. All the greatest people who ever
> lived have been telling us about it for five thou-
> sand years and yet you'd be surprised how people
> are always losing hold of it. There's something
> way down deep that's eternal about every human
> being.[20]

*8. How much should we mourn the death of a
friend or loved one?*

In the Doctrine and Covenants, Section 42, verse
45 it reads:

---

[20]Evans, Richard Evans' Quote Book, p. 115.

> Thou shalt live together in love, insomuch that thou shalt weep for the loss of them that die, and more especially for those that have not hope of a glorious resurrection.

It is clear that the Lord *expects* us to weep for the loss of loved ones who pass away.

> We mourn; we sorrow for our loved ones that go — our wives, our husbands, our children, our parents; we sorrow for them; and it is well and proper that we should mourn for them and shed tears for the loss, for it is our loss; but it is their gain.[21]

An unknown author put it this way: "The only way to take the sorrow out of death is to take love out of life."

Although it is proper to weep or mourn for the death of a friend or loved one, we should do so because we will miss our association with them and not because we perceive death to be a monster of permanent destruction. No such mourning should be prolonged or convey a hopelessness regarding the future. We need to remember that: "Death is not a subject for mourning when it is followed by immortality."[22]

Finally, let's turn to President Joseph F. Smith, who said:

---

[21] Francis M. Lyman, in Conference Report, (Oct. 1909), p. 18.

[22] Cicero as quoted by Evans, *Richard L. Evans' Quote Book*, p. 116.

It is true, I am weak enough to weep at the death of my friends and kindred. I may shed tears when I see the grief of others. I have sympathy in my soul for the children of men. I can weep with them when they weep: I can rejoice with them when they rejoice; but I have no cause to mourn, nor to be sad because death comes into the world.[23]

9. Is there such a thing as untimely or unjust death?

Dealing emotionally with the loss of a loved one whose death seems to have been premature or accidental is one of the most difficult challenges of life. However, if we suggest that early death is a tragedy, we are saying that mortality is better than early entrance into the spirit world. With an enlarged perspective, we can accept early death as a blessing.

It matters not at what hour the righteous fall asleep.
— Death cannot come *untimely* to him who is fit to die.
— The less of this cold world the more of heaven, the briefer life, the earlier immortality.[24]

The Prophet Joseph Smith, who lost five of his own natural children and one that was adopted, gave this counsel:

---

[23]Joseph F. Smith, in Conference Report, (Oct. 1899), pp. 20-21..

[24]Milman as quoted by Evans, *Richard Evans' Quote Book*, p. 116.

The Lord takes many away, even in infancy, that they may escape the envy of man, and the sorrows and evils of this present world; they were too pure, too lovely, to live on earth; therefore, if rightly considered, instead of mourning we would have reason to rejoice as they are delivered from evil, and we shall soon have them again...The only difference between the old and young dying is, one lives longer in heaven and eternal light and glory than the other, and is freed a little sooner from this miserable wicked world.[25]

President Spencer W. Kimball explained that even in death we have a degree of free agency. There are some cases where death *is* untimely, because of the actions of the person who has died. In these situations, the responsibility for mortality's early end lies with the individual.

I am confident that there is a time to die, but I believe also that many people die before "their time" because they are careless, abuse their bodies, take unnecessary chances, or expose themselves to hazards, accidents, and sickness. In Ecclesiastes 7:17 we find this statement, "Be not over much wicked, neither be thou foolish: why shouldest thou die before thy time?" ...God controls our lives, guides and blesses us, but gives us our agency. We may live our lives in accordance

---

[25]Joseph Smith, *History of the Church*, Salt Lake City, Ut.: Deseret Book, 2nd ed., 1959, Vol 4, pp. 553-554

with His plan for us or we may foolishly shorten or terminate them.[26]

Although free agency is sometimes involved, it is important to recognize when there is no guilt associated with death. Parents often feel responsible for the death of an infant or child or blame the Lord for taking them. In regard to these emotions, Elder Hyrum G. Smith said:

> Do not accuse the Lord of taking your little ones from you, nor feel that you have committed any great sin, that those little ones are taken from you...[27]

And President Wilford Woodruff continued:

> Your children are taken away and you cannot help it; we cannot any of us help it; there is no censure to be given to parents when they do the best they can. A mother should not be censured because she cannot save her sick child and we have to leave these things in the hand of God.[28]

The following remarkable story told by President Heber J. Grant gives great comfort and perspective on seemingly untimely or unjust death. His experience provides us with an appropriate and valiant model in accepting personal loss:

---

[26]Spencer W. Kimball, "Tragedy or Destiny," Salt Lake City, Ut.: Deseret Book, Co., 1977, p. 9.

[27]Hyrum G. Smith, in Conference Report, (Apr. 1917), pp. 70-71.

[28]Burton, *For They Shall Be Comforted*, p. 60.

About an hour before my wife died, I called my children into her room and told them that their mother was dying and for them to bid her good-bye. One of the little girls, about twelve years of age, said to me: "Papa, I do not want mamma to die...I want you to lay hands upon my mamma and heal her." I told my little girl that we all had to die sometime and that I felt assured in my heart that her mother's time had arrived; and she and the rest of the children left the room. I knelt down by the bed of my wife (who by this time had lost consciousness) and I told the Lord I acknowledged His hand in life, in death, in joy, in sorrow, in prosperity or adversity. I thanked him for the knowledge I had that my wife belonged to me for all eternity...I supplicated the Lord with all the strength that I possessed, that he would give to that little girl of mine a knowledge that it was His mind and will that her mamma should die.

Within an hour my wife passed away, and I called the children back into the room. My little boy about five and a half years of age was weeping bitterly, and the little girl who was twelve years of age, took him in her arms and said: "Do not weep, the voice of the Lord from heaven has said to me, 'In the death of your mamma the will of the Lord shall be done."

I have been blessed with only two sons. One of them died at five years of age and the other at seven. My last son died of a hip disease. I had built great hopes that he would live to spread the Gospel at home and abroad and be an honor to me. About an hour before he died I had a dream that his mother, who was dead, came for him, and that she brought with her a messenger, and she told this messenger to take the boy while I was asleep; and in the dream I thought I awoke and I succeeded in getting him away from the messenger who had come to take him, and in doing so I dreamed that I stumbled and fell upon him...I dreamed that I fell upon his sore hip, and the terrible cries and anguish of the child drove me nearly wild. I could not stand it and I jumped up and ran out of the house so as not to hear his distress. I dreamed that after running out of the house I met Brother Joseph E. Taylor and told him of these things.

He said: "Well, Heber, do you know what I would do if my wife came for one of her children — I would not struggle for that child; I would not oppose her taking that child away." I said, "I believe you are right, Brother Taylor, and if she comes again, she shall have the boy without any protest on my part."

After coming to that conclusion, I was (awakened) by my brother, B.F. Grant, who was staying that night with us, helping us to watch over the sick boy. He called me into the room and told me that my child was dying. I went in the front room and sat down. There was a vacant chair between me and my wife who is now living, and I felt the presence of that boy's deceased mother, sitting in that chair. I did not tell anybody what I felt, but I turned to my living wife and said: "Do you feel anything strange?" She said: "Yes, I feel assurance that Heber's mother is sitting between us, waiting to take him away."

I believe that I am naturally affectionate and sympathetic and that I shed tears for my friends — tears of joy for their success and tears of sorrow for their misfortunes. But I sat by the deathbed of my little boy and saw him die without shedding a tear. My living wife, my brother, and I, upon that occasion experienced a sweet peaceful and heavenly influence in my home as great as I have ever experienced in my life; and no person can tell me that every other Latter-day Saint that has knowledge of the Gospel in his heart and soul, can really mourn for his loved ones, only in the loss of their society here in this life.[29]

---

[29] Burton, *For They Shall Be Comforted*, p. 65-68.

SECTION II

Contact With Spirits

2

Family Concern

We know through the teachings of our prophets that the spirit world is very near, only separated from us by a veil.[1] In agreement with this principle, experiences with the death transition clearly reveal the nearness of the spirit world and its inhabitants.

My mother was critically ill with stomach cancer, and her sister Sarah and I went to be with her in the hospital in Brigham City, Utah. The day before she died, she got talking to her own mother (my grandmother), who was dead. Sarah and I didn't disturb her as she gave a report on

---

[1] Brigham Young taught that the spirit world "is incorporated within this celestial system. Can you see it with your natural eyes? No. Can you see spirits in this room? No. Suppose the Lord should touch your eyes that you might see, could you then see the spirits? Yes, as plainly as you now see bodies, as did the servant of Elijah. If the Lord would permit it, and it was His will that it should be done, you could see the spirits that have departed from this world as plainly as you now see bodies with your natural eyes." --Brigham Young, Journal of Discourses (JD), 3:368.

her children and brothers and sisters to her
mother. Hearing this was like listening to a one-
way telephone conversation.

When she had finished, my mother told
Sarah that their mother had been to see her.
Then she told me she was ready to go.

Later she started talking again to someone we
couldn't see. She was referring to childhood experiences that only Sarah could remember. Then
she stopped and said,

"Sarah, Mother came and talked to me. We
talked about you and [this brother, and that
brother]."

Her stake president was also her doctor. He
felt she could be kept alive indefinitely on machines, but if she were taken off life support, she
might die within six hours or she might linger
for days.

The nine children in our family decided that
she should be taken off the machines. We gathered around her as the doctor unplugged the
support system, and she was given a blessing of
release. The doctor had not gone three steps from
her bed before she died.

Although dying is something each person does
for and by himself, experience reveals that it is not a
lonely transition. Elder Charles A. Callis suggests
that death is a time when our minds see beyond
this world and its limitations in a flash. He says, "I
have been with Elders who died in the mission
field, and a moment or two before they departed
this life their faces have been overspread with a
gleam of recognition of beings not of this world;
they have uttered the names of loved ones long

since gone and then have peacefully gone to their eternal rest."[2]

Near death experiences consistently suggest that as each of us leaves the companionship of the physical world and discovers the presence of other spirits, the most overwhelming discovery we will make is how much these spirits care about us. The following experience shows the importance of their love.

When I was about five years old, our neighbors in Baton Rouge, Louisiana, sent the missionaries over to see us. My mother let them in, and my parents were consequently converted. My sister and I grew up in the Church, and when I graduated, after attending Ricks College for a time, I went on a mission.

I had been serving for about six months in the San Diego, California Mission when I became very depressed. All my life I had been protected from the real world. Even my experiences with worldly things as a high school student had not awakened me to the darkness and real hell this life can be for many people. It was not until I went on my mission that I began to feel the true weight of adversity and the pervasive powers of light and darkness, goodness and evil, love and hate inside myself and everyone around me.

I began to sense, as I never had before, the war that is constantly being waged against us. I sup-

---

[2]Charles A. Callis, *Fundamentals of Religion.* Salt Lake City, Ut.: Deseret Book Co., 1945, p. 88. Another excellent example of this is Joseph Smith's description of his brother Alvin's death, "Alvin was one of the soberest of men, and when he died the angel of the Lord visited him in his last moments" (Documentary History of The Church 5:127).

pose the devil wanted more than ever to wrap
me in his chains, for I was on a mission against
him. It seemed that he must have had his way,
for I succumbed to depression and dis-
couragement deeper than I had ever imagined.

One preparation day, I desperately wanted to
forget it all — to get away from everything just
for a day. Contrary to my own moral convictions,
I chose to escape by drinking alcohol. My companion consented, seeing the desperate state I was
in, but did not participate. He patiently attended
me as I swallowed drink after drink. But to my
surprise, my troubles did not float away as I had
supposed they would. As my worries intensified,
I concluded it would only take more to make me
forget. Ignorant of the fact that my moral development was going to keep me from finding release in selfish indulgence, I continued to guzzle
still more.

Eventually, I drank so much that my bowels
began to cringe with excruciating pain. Never in
my life had I experience such agony. My companion and I had been walking and were on the out-
skirts of our apartment complex, when suddenly
the pain became so overwhelming that I doubled
over, grasping my stomach and screaming. My
companion bent and lifted me to his shoulder,
carrying me all the way to our apartment. The
Christology of that act filled my mind and senses
until he laid me upon my bed.

By the time we reached our rooms, my
screaming had given way to sobbing out the
words, 'I want to die! I want to die! I want to die!"

As I curled on my bed in the torment of my
pain, the memory of my father's deceased mother

crossed my mind and I said, "Grandma. I want to see Grandma."

I had been gasping because of the pain, but somehow I just gave up and felt my last breath leave my mouth. At that instant, all the pain was gone, and I was flying at an enormous speed through darkness into a light. My flight stopped just within the darkness, and I gazed into the light, sensing the power that emanated from it.

My Grandmother appeared within this wonderful, pure light. She was smiling, totally at peace and harmony with herself and her surroundings; an indescribable purity and unconditional love emanated from her and the light toward me. Grandma spoke no words. The love said everything. her eyes were filled with deepest compassion, and I was swept with overwhelming longing to enter into the light with her, but I heard sacred words of command from the world I had left.

"By the power of the Holy Melchizedek Priesthood and in the name of Jesus Christ, I command you to come back to life."

The instant I heard these words, though I had been far, far away, I found myself suddenly back in my body. The intense pain clamped at my stomach, and I could feel my companion's hands upon my head. He finished giving me the blessing, promising that the hurt would subside, that I would rest well, and upon awakening all would be normal. I did awaken, physically the same as if the whole occurrence had never happened, and through the blessings of our Father in Heaven, I am able to tell about this experience today.

My depression did not get much better at first. I was very grateful for life in some ways, but I was also aware of the world beyond. This world seemed dark, like hell in comparison. I didn't really see the world beyond as much as I sensed it. I just saw my grandmother and the light, but the light in her and the power and love that was there was enough. There was no need to see more. I wanted to be there, and I never wanted to come back here again.

Over time I can see the impact of this experience more clearly. Understanding the trials of this world was something I needed to work through. Taking them away wouldn't have helped me, but knowing they are not forever gives me strength. I am so grateful for what happened, and I am not the least bit afraid to die. The difference now is that I have a wife and little baby boy, and I want to be here for them. But if the Lord wanted to take me, I would not be afraid to go.

I imagine some people could assign psychological explanations and/or the influence of liquor to discredit what I have explained, but it is my firm and undeniable testimony that what happened to me was real. My spirit left my body and I did in reality glimpse the glory and the wonder of the other side. To deny it or that I was brought back to life by the authority of the priesthood would be to deny Him...our God.

Experiences like the one we have just shared, where no words are spoken, are supported by their sheer number. The pattern that emerges is that the experiences are the result of a deceased person's interest in and concern for friends or family who are still living. Not all encounters with deceased family

members require an out-of-the-body situation, as in
the following example:

> One night when I was a little boy, I woke up
> with the distinct sensation that I was not alone.
> No one was in my room, but as I looked toward
> the door, I saw a woman come down the hall
> from my parents' room and in the door of my
> own room. To me, the woman looked like a fe-
> male version of my father. You can tell when you
> are not dreaming, and I knew I was not. She
> walked right up to my bed, and bending over it,
> peered at me. Terrified, I did what I think any
> child would do — I threw the covers over my
> head. When I was brave enough to put them
> down, she was gone.
>
> As I think about it now, she didn't look scary
> and she did nothing to frighten me, but I was
> afraid of something so unknown. She looked just
> like any person, except I could tell that she had no
> body. She was a spirit, or a ghost as I would have
> put it then.
>
> The next day my parents were informed that
> my father's sister had passed away during the
> night, at the same time I had seen the woman.
> My visitor had to have been my aunt, whom I
> had not met.

Often when a spirit appears, it is for the special
purpose of comforting loved ones. Words may not
be necessary, but at other times they are used. Regardless of the communication method, experiences like these reveal that the deceased consis-

tently wish the living would not mourn them too deeply.[3]

My grandmother lived alone when she was well into her nineties. My grandfather had preceded her in death, and my mother took the responsibility of caring for her. It was a strain and a continual worry because we were afraid something would happen and that no one would know since she was alone in her own house. Grandma had been very afraid of dying. It almost seemed that her fear was keeping her alive. The strain of all this weighed heavily on my mother. When I had completed my mission in Taiwan, my mother and father made arrangements to come and pick me up there. My mother was very worried that something would happen to Grandma, but she found someone Grandma liked to come and stay with her; and although she was nervous about it, she flew to Taiwan. We all encouraged her to make the trip because she needed the break.

My parents had not been away long when the news came that Grandma had passed away. My mother, feeling it was all her fault, was distressed and feared Grandma had felt deserted and died because of it. The entire family felt responsible for Grandma's death and we were all upset over it. Knowing how much Grandma feared death, we hoped she had gone peacefully and willingly. Despite assurances from the lady who had taken care of her, we were concerned.

---

[3]See Chapter I, question #8.

One night around the time of the funeral, my fourteen-year-old niece woke to find Grandmother and Grandfather standing at the foot of her bed. Grandma told her, "It's all right. Everything is fine." Then they were gone. I guess we were all just so upset over it that Grandma couldn't reassure any of the rest of us.

Cases like this one, where recently departed spirits appear to mortal family members to console, reassure, or give comfort, are the most common type of contact with the next world. The spirits are concerned about our anxiety over their death, and though it is normal to mourn for loved ones who have passed on, it is distressing for both them and us if we remain inconsolable and distraught. While it is true that "We understand death the first time he puts his hand upon one whom we love,"[4] it is also true that "Each departed friend is a magnet that attracts us to the next world."[5] We can be sure that the more loss we suffer in this life, the more vast our reunion will be in the next.

The consistent theme in experiences dealing with spirits is the predominance and concern family members beyond the veil have for us. In almost every case, there is a sense of comfort.[6] In fact, com-

---

[4]Madam de Stael as quoted by Evans, *Richard Evans' Quote Book*, p. 121.

[5]Jean Paul Richter as quoted by Evans, *Richard Evans' Quote Book*, p. 126.

[6]When it is absent, the individual explaining what happened, usually remarks that the encounter was so brief he could not tell what the occurrence meant, or that his own fear and/or surprise at the situation made it impossible to discern the spirit's feelings. Obviously, the exception to this would be encounters with evil spirits--a subject we are not addressing here.

fort appears to be the reason for most contact with the spirit world, including this case with Rodney:

Several days after extensive surgery in 1972, I was still in the intensive care unit of the St. Benedict's Hospital in Ogden, Utah. I had not responded or awakened from the surgery and was not expected to live through the night.

However, I was aware of the happenings in the ICU. The evening nurse had checked my monitors and set me in for the night. In severe pain, I watched the lights on the monitor. When the hurt gradually grew worse, I began to feel very cold.

As I felt myself being lifted from my body, the pain subsided. The coldness that had clasped me gave way to warmth, and I looked down on my body as I was lifted up.

My father was with me, though he had been dead for twenty-seven years. I felt his presence more than I saw him, but I did observe that there was green grass scattered with delicate purple flowers, and exquisite little birds were singing. I was aware of many people, most of whom I knew. I was happy to be with them, yet I was excited above all about being with my father once again.

Dad and I visited for a long time, though I cannot remember what we talked about because I was so overwhelmed with the wonderful feeling all around me. After a time, however, I was told that I must go back. I was very reluctant and wanted to stay, but I new clearly that I must go.

I was brought back through the upper corner of the room above my body. I looked down and saw it lying on the bed with the monitor machines beside it. Slowly I settled into my body again, with all its pain and the terrible cold. I was awake when the nurse came in and said, "Oh, Mr. Jensen, you must feel good, you rested so well we didn't even disturb you to take your blood pressure."

I was intensely sorry about having to return and fervently hoped that my father would come back for me all that next day.

Rodney lived and suffered for seven more years. During that time, he bore testimony that any fear of death or doubt of a hereafter was completely wiped away in this more sure testimony of eternal life. Although his account was of an out-of-the-body situation and the next experience is of a visitation, both cases describe parents' love as they visit their suffering children to relieve pain, at least momentarily, and to bring solace.

In 1973, my mother was really sick in Mexico while I was living at the border in Tijuana. Since she was not a member of the Church, I wanted her to know of my testimony so that when she was taught the gospel in Paradise, she would know that I believed it. This was why I wrote her a letter, asking her to please listen to the missionaries there. But I was far away from the post office and I had two little ones. Because the weather was bad, I waited for an easier time to send the letter.

The day after I finally sent the letter, I received one from my brother telling me my mother had died. This meant that my mother did not get my letter in time. I was really upset with myself because I hadn't mailed the letter sooner. I cried a lot about it and felt the need to pray because I had not made a big enough effort to tell my mother about the gospel. My crying and praying that she could know even though I had failed went on for three days. I could not forgive myself.

When I went to sleep on the third night after my brother's letter came, I had a dream, but it was not like a regular dream. It was a vision, a vision dreaming. I don't know exactly how to explain it, but I saw myself looking up, and I saw this light become bigger and bigger until I saw my mother standing in the middle of the room.

Her dress was white and the light around her was bright, but I could still see her face. She was beautiful, younger, and happy. She had suffered with cancer for twenty years before death. Although her body had been worn out by the cancer and by seventy-five years of life, her face was now beautiful. Her clothing was not like a robe, but more like a tunic. I can't remember the sleeves, but the robe fell straight. That was just the style of long dress she liked to wear when she was alive, yet she had never worn white. This was the only time I ever saw her in white.

She said, "I was allowed to come, and tell you not to be worried about me. I don't suffer any more and I am very happy." I distinctly remember that she spoke with me by telepathy, not words. She made it very clear that there is a certain authority in the spirit world that allowed her to come.

We talked for a little while, though I cannot remember what we said. Then she explained that she needed to go and that she was planning to visit my brother also. The light began to grow smaller and smaller, and then I woke up.

She didn't tell me anything about the Church and in that respect I still worry a bit, but I felt so relieved and happy when I woke up. Seeing her dressed in white made me feel that she is in Paradise.

Joseph Smith said that the spirits whom we held dear in mortality and who are sent to minister unto us, are not far from us. They know and understand our thoughts, feelings, and motions, and are often pained by them.[7] Our deceased family is much larger than our living family, and their presence and concern for us is greater than we often realize. If we were actually aware of how many individuals are pulling for us, the mountains of this life would seem far less steep.

---

[7]Joseph Smith, *History of the Church,* Vol. 6, p. 52.

Questions and Answers

1. *Who are we most likely to meet during a near death experience or spiritual manifestation?*

The Prophet Joseph Smith stated:

> I have a father, brothers, children, and friends who have gone to a world of spirits. They are only absent for a moment. They are in the spirit, and we shall soon meet again. The time will arrive when the trumpet shall sound. When we depart, we shall hail our mothers, fathers, friends, and all whom we love who have fallen asleep in Jesus...The expectation of seeing my friends in the morning of the resurrection cheers my soul and makes me bear up against the evils of life. It is like their taking a long journey, and on their return we meet them with increased joy.[8]

Although the first spirit a dying person meets may be a messenger or a close friend, the predominance of family members is striking. Each of the spiritual manifestations described in this chapter was centered on a relative and that, indeed, is who we are most likely to meet. But because every individual's experience is unique, predicting *which* family member will come is impossible on a general basis.

---

[8]Joseph Smith, *History of the Church*, Vol. 5, p. 362.

> And so for me there is no sting of death,
> And so the grave has lost its victory.
> It is but crossing — with abated breath
> And white, set face — a little strip of sea
> To find the loved ones waiting on the shore,
> More beautiful, more precious than before.[9]

2. What is the significance of the bright light described in so many of the accounts?

The Prophet Isaiah seems to have associated a bright light with death when he said:

> The people that walked in darkness have seen a great light: they that dwell in the land of the shadow of death, upon them hath the light shined. (Isaiah 9:2)

The bright light seems to come from the presence of angels (resurrected personages, having bodies of flesh and bones),[10] the spirits of just men made perfect (spirits who are not resurrected, but will inherit the same glory),[11] or the Savior, Jesus Christ.

In his study, Dr. Moody says that the bright light is the most incredible common element of the death experience. There was no doubt in every case that it was a being of light, but the descriptions varied with each individual and seemed to be largely a

---

[9]Evans, *Richard Evans' Quote Book*, p. 119.

[10]Joseph Smith, Jr., D&C 129:2.

[11]D&C 129:3.

function of religious background because of the
varied expectations and perceptions different back-
grounds cause. A Jewish person would identify it as
an angel, whereas a Christian would be more likely
to identify it as the Savior.[12] We have interviewed
many Latter-day Saints, and they generally describe
the being of light as a deceased family member (see
question #1, this section). In nearly every case, the
being is a guide.[13]

As a final description of the being of light, we
turn to Dr. George Ritchie's experience:

> I wasn't sure when the light in the room be-
> gan to change; suddenly I was aware that it was
> brighter, a lot brighter, than it had been. I whirled
> to look at the night light on the bedside table.
> Surely a single fifteen watt bulb couldn't turn out
> that much light?
>
> I stared in astonishment as the brightness in-
> creased, coming from nowhere, seeming to shine
> everywhere at once. All the light bulbs in the
> ward couldn't give off that much light. All the
> bulbs in the world couldn't! It was impossibly
> bright: It was like a million welder's lamps all

---

[12]Moody, *Life After Life*, pp. 58-60.

[13]The absence of light and the presence of darkness around a spirit indicates the
forces of evil. Elder Parley P. Pratt, speaking of two kinds of disembodied
spirits said, "Persons who have departed this life, and have not yet been
raised from the dead are spirits. There are two kinds, viz. good and evil."
He explained that the good spirits minister to the heirs of salvation both in
this world and in the world of spirits, but in appearing to men, they cannot
hide their glory, or brightness, which is greater than that of the sun. He
goes on to say, "Spirits not worthy to be glorified will appear without this
brilliant halo, and although they often attempt to pass as angels of light,
there is more or less darkness about them. So it is with Satan and his hosts
who have not been embodied. Parley P. Pratt, *Key to the Science of
Theology*, 10th ed., Salt Lake City, Ut.: Deseret Book, 1966, p. 116.

blazing at once. And right in the middle of my amazement came a prosaic thought probably born of some biology lecture back at the university: "I'm glad I don't have physical eyes at the moment," I thought. "This light would destroy the retina in a tenth of a second."[14]

3. How do spirits and mortals communicate?

There appear to be many ways for spirits and mortals to communicate: thought patterns through dreams, telepathic communication in out-of-the-body experiences, and verbal messages.

Dreams: There are over thirty significant scriptural references in the Standard Works where communication from beyond the veil occurred through dreams. One of the more familiar examples is found in the gospel of Matthew, where Joseph is warned in a dream to take Mary and Jesus and flee into Egypt to escape the wrath of King Herod, and then to return once again following his death.

Besides scriptural examples, we have many contemporary accounts where information is communicated in dreams. Based on the experiences cited in this chapter alone, we can see that the knowledge is given telepathically, or from spirit to spirit.

Elder Parley P. Pratt explained communication between mortals and spirits through dreams in this way:

---

[14]George G. Ritchie, M.D.,*Return from Tomorrow*, Old Tappan, New Jersey: Fleming H. Revell Co., 1978, p. 48.

When the outward organs of thought and
perception are released from their activity, the
nerves unstrung, and the whole of mortal hu-
manity lies hushed in quite slumbers, in order to
renew its strength and vigor, it is then that the
spiritual organs are at liberty in a certain degree,
to assume their wonted functions, to recall some
faint outlines, some confused and half-defined
recollections, of that heavenly world, and those
endearing scenes of their former estate, from
which they have descended in order to obtain
and mature a tabernacle of flesh.

In this situation, we frequently hold a com-
munion with our departed father, mother,
brother, sister, son or daughter; or with the former husband or wife of our bosom, whose affec-
tion for us, being rooted and grounded in the
eternal elements, or issuing from under the
sanctuary of love's eternal fountain, can never be
lessened or diminished by death, distance of
space, or length of years.[15]

Out-of-the-Body Experiences: It is difficult for an
individual to describe the process of communication during his or her out-of-the-body experience
because it is telepathic, something we do not often
refer to. For example, in one experience in this
chapter, we were told: "Grandma spoke no words.
The love said everything..."

Dr. Moody suggests that in communicating with
the being of light, "direct, unimpeded transfer of
thoughts takes place, and in such a clear way that

---

[15]Parley P. Pratt, *Key to the Science of Theology*, pp. 120-122.

there is no possibility whatsoever either of misunderstanding or of lying...″[16]

Visitations: During visitations, most communication seems to be verbal. For example, comfort was given to a young mother who had lost her beloved daughter to sudden infant death syndrome. On the third night she plead for peace of mind that she could stop blaming herself. Then, she recalls:

> In a half-awakened, half-sleeping state, I became aware of someone standing behind me. I turned to see a young woman seemingly about twenty years old with long dark hair. I've since tried hard to recall what the looked like, but all I can remember is that she was beautiful. She spoke only one word: "Mother!" But as she said it I felt immediate relief.[17]

There are many scriptural accounts of spirits or resurrected beings communicating with mortals. Some of these are very familiar to Latter-day Saints:

> And [Christ] was transfigured before them: and his face did shine as the sun, and his raiment was white as the light. And, behold, there appeared unto them Moses and Elias (Elijah) talking with him. (Matt. 17:2,3).

> When the light rested upon me I saw two Personages, whose brightness and glory defy all

---

[16]Moody, *Life After Death*, p. 60.

[17]Avril Marie Campbell, "When Julie Died," *Ensign*, Aug. 1977, pp. 56-57.

description, standing above me in the air. One of them spake unto me, calling me by name and said, pointing to the other — This is my Beloved Son, Hear Him! (JS-H 1:17)

While I was thus in the act of calling upon God, I discovered a light appearing in my room, which continued to increase until the room was lighter than at noonday, when immediately a personage appeared at my bedside, standing in the air, for his feet did not touch the floor...He called me by name, and said unto me that he was a messenger from the presence of God to me, and that his name was Moroni...(JS-H 1:30,33)

4. What do departed spirits know about us?

Righteous spirits know a great deal about us and — more often than we realize — they are allowed to return from paradise to earth. Normally they return to those whom they have known in mortality in order to fulfill a righteous purpose. Joseph Smith taught:

There are no angels who minister to this earth but those who do belong or have belonged to it. Hence when messengers are sent to minister to the inhabitants of this earth, they are not strangers, but from the ranks of our kindred, friends, and brothers and sisters and friends who have passed away from this earth, having been faithful, and worthy to enjoy these rights and privileges, may have a mission given them to visit their relatives and friends upon the earth again, bringing from the divine Presence messages of love, of warning, or reproof and instruction, to those whom they had learned to love in the flesh.[18]

Generally then, spirits who minister to us are well acquainted with us. Heber C. Kimball enlarged upon this idea when he said:

> Some may think the Almighty does not see their doings, but if He does not, the angels and ministering spirits do. They see you and your works, and I have no doubt but that they occasionally communicate your conduct to the Father, or to the Son, or to Joseph, or to Peter, or to someone who holds the keys in connection with them. Perhaps there are some who do not believe in spirits, but I know that they exist and visit the earth.[19]

President Joseph F. Smith taught that those who had been chosen to lay the foundation for God's work would not be deprived in the spirit world of looking down on the results of their labors,[20] and Wilford Woodruff said that "the whole spirit world is watching your labor and your works."[21] With this in mind, it is not surprising to think that our loved ones who have gone beyond know about us and our concerns.

---

[18]Joseph F. Smith, *Gospel Doctrine*, Salt Lake City, Ut.: Deseret Book Co., 1919, pp. 435-436.

[19]Heber C. Kimball, *Journal of Discourses*, 3:228-9, March 2, 1856.

[20]Joseph F. Smith, in Conference Report (Apr. 1916), pp. 2-3.

[21]Wilford Woodruff, in Conference Report (Apr. 1880), p. 11.

One example of this is Eliza Dean Neville's experience. She was visited by her father who revealed his knowledge about the mortal world by expressing concern for his children on earth. He said that he could not accomplish his work because of the attitude of his children. Eliza replied:

> "Why father, your children have never done anything very bad have they?" He replied, "They are dying spiritually. Look and I'll show you!" Then she saw that they were not united, but were standing with their backs toward each other. He explained: "Some are complaining about paying their tithing; they say the Church is better off than they are. If they could only see!"[22]

Clearly, nearly all experiences of this nature demonstrate interest, concern, and knowledge of our future by our family members in the spirit world.

5. How are spirits dressed?

The clothing spirits wear is perceived in different ways. John the Revelator described the dress of the righteous spirits who had been slain for their testimony of Jesus, explaining that white robes were given to every one of them.

Joseph Smith gave one of the most detailed descriptions of a post-mortal being when he described the attire of the Angel Moroni in these words:

---

[22]Duane S. Crowther, *Life Everlasting*. Salt Lake City, Ut.: Bookcraft, Inc., 1967, p. 111.

He had on a loose robe of most exquisite whiteness. It was a whiteness beyond anything earthly I had ever seen; nor do I believe that any earthly thing could be made to appear so exceedingly white and brilliant. His hands were naked, and his arms also, a little above the wrist; so, also, were his feet naked, as were his legs, a little above the ankles. His head and neck were also bare. I could discover that he had no other clothing on but this robe, as it was open, so that I could see into his bosom. (JS-H 1:31)

Most accounts, like Ligia's in this chapter, describe white apparel similar to Moroni's. Perhaps exceptions could be explained as a subjective perception of an indescribable experience, or as the appearance of a spirit in clothing that would make him more recognizable to the person seeing him. An example of this would be Ella Jensen's description of her uncle:

The people were all dressed in white or cream, excepting Uncle Hans Jensen, who had on his dark clothes and long rubber boots, the things he wore when he was drowned in the Snake River in Idaho.[23]

Before his death, Alonzo Hinckley described "Three heavenly messengers dressed in the robes of

---

[23]Gordon T. Allred, *If A Man Die*, Salt Lake City, Ut.: Bookcraft Inc., 1964, p. 121.

the Holy Priesthood,"[24] while in Heber Q. Hales' account in the Epilogue, we will read that he saw a variety of clothing styles, including soldiers in uniform.

6. *Is age a characteristic of spirits?*

President Joseph F. Smith taught:

> The spirits of our children are immortal before they come to us, and their spirits, after bodily death, are like they were before they came. They are as they would have appeared if they had lived in the flesh, to grow to maturity, or to develop their physical bodies to the full stature of their spirits. If you see one of your children that has passed away, it may appear to you in the form in which you would recognize it, the form of childhood; but if it came to you as a messenger bearing some important truth, it would perhaps come as the spirit of Bishop Edward Hunter's son (who died when a little child) came to him, in the stature of full-grown manhood, and revealed himself to his father, and said, "I am your son."[25]

Several examples of spirits appearing as children can be found in chapters to come. Ella Jensen reported her experience:

> Finally I reached the end of that long room. I opened a door and went into another room filled

---

[24]Bryant S. Hinckley, *The Faith of Our Pioneer Fathers*, Salt Lake City, Ut.: Deseret Book Co., 1959, p. 236.

[25]Joseph F. Smith, *Gospel Doctrine*, p. 455.

with children. They were all arrayed in perfect
order, the smallest ones first, then the larger
ones, according to age and size, in back rows all
around the room. They seemed to be convened
in a sort of a Primary or a Sunday School
presided over by aunt Eliza R. Snow. There were
hundreds of small children.[26]

It is important to remember that Ella was a Sunday School teacher when she died, and perhaps
perceived her spirit world experience in terms of
things she was familiar with. We should bear in
mind the importance of perceptions and the differ-
ing purposes for experiences when we read about
Heber Q. Hale's surprise at finding no babies in
arms. He said:

(I felt) quite contented that mothers will again
receive into their arms the children who died in
infancy and will be fully satisfied; but the fact remains that entrance into the world of spirits is
not an inhibition of growth, but the greater opportunity for development. Babies are adult spirits in infant bodies.[27]

Wilford Woodruff said:

Children are taken away in their infancy, and
they go to the spirit world...Our children will be
restored to us as they are laid down if we, their

---

[26]Allred, *If A Man Die*, p. 121.

[27]Heber Q. Hale, "A Heavenly Manifestation by Heber Q. Hale, President of
Boise Stake," unpublished manuscript.

parents, keep the faith and prove ourselves worthy to obtain eternal life.[28]

In light of the information available, it seems that a spirit may appear the age that is easiest to recognize, or will best fulfill the purpose of his visit. However, we can make no generalization about the age of spirits.

7. *Is there interaction between post-mortal and pre-mortal spirits?*

Regarding his out-of-the-body experience, Henry Zollinger said:

> My Guide took me and showed me the spirits of the children that would yet come to my family, if we would be faithful. They were full grown, but not in the same sphere as those which had lived upon this earth.[29]

This experience suggests that there may not be any association between premortal and postmortal spirits since they are in different spheres.

---

[28]Burton, *For They Shall Be Comforted*, p. 60.

[29]As cited in *Life Everlasting* by Duane Crowther, Salt Lake City, Ut.: Bookcraft, Inc., 1967, p. 39.

3

Involvement

Often a brush with death and/or the spirit world eventually leads to contact with someone from the other side. This was the case for Lloyd, who glimpsed the next world on a snowy February morning, thirty feet above the ground.

I was traveling to Holbrook, Idaho, on the 28th of February in 1969, to do some business for my grain brokerage. My wife and I had been feeling the imminence of death and had talked about it before I left. Because our dear friend Melburn Archibald had been killed only two days before, we had been pondering what a predicament it would put us in if something happened to one of us. Melburn had been instrumental in developing my testimony of the gospel and activating me in the Church. Two days prior to my trip, while busy with his business of machinery sales, he had crossed a railroad track at such an angle that he did not see the oncoming locomotive until it struck his truck broadside. He was killed instantly.

I left home in very low spirits. The loss of my dear friend caused me to reminisce as I drove through the fifteen inches of new snow covering the highways. When I arrived in Holbrook, I proceeded to secure the wheat sample I had come for. The tool I used was made of three-foot lengths of pipe, put together to reach the bottom of the grain bin and bring up a sample.

As it was very cold, I dressed in several layers of clothing, including gloves and overshoes. The steel silo was only half-full, so I went up the ladder on the side, opened the lid, and climbed down in. I put four lengths of pipe together and got a sample. Then, as I put the wheat in a bag, I thought to myself that there was no reason to take the pipes apart since I needed to cross over to the neighbor's and get a sample of his wheat as well. I climbed up the ladder on the inside of the silo and turned to get footing on the top rungs of the ladder on the outside.

I started down the ladder, pulling the lengths of pipe up out of the silo as I went. The pipes touched a wire, and I was suddenly struck with a 12,000-volt charge of electricity. I was literally on fire, and as the force shot me back in the air, the entire countryside spread before my view.

I can't put words to what happened next. Into my mind flashed my wife and our seven children. I was filled with an intense desire to live. *I do not want to die! Please, Lord, could you spare me?* Even before a second passed, these thoughts were so intense in my mind that I begged and pleaded with all my soul.

Then I saw a personage in front of me — my friend, Melburn Archibald. He was vivid, distinct, and real. That was the last thing I remember.

I woke up a few days later in the hospital and the first thought I had was a rerun of this experience, of seeing my dead friend. I didn't just think it over once and forget it, because it didn't leave my mind. The whole occurrence was a very spiritual experience. Melburn was just there — no voice, no actions at all. I did see him; I know I did. I couldn't put this experience off as a dream or fluke caused by fear — it was real.

I got to the hospital miraculously. A fellow who was plowing snow with a road patrol saw me as he rounded the point of the mountain. Actually, what he saw was a ball of fire, and then he heard the explosion. Somehow, my leg had become caught in the ladder, and I was hanging there, like on monkey-bars, but unconscious, thirty feet above the ground. The man with the road patrol only weighed 150 pounds, but he climbed the ladder and slung me over his shoulder. Then he carried me down to a safe position on the ground before going for help.

Later, in the court room, he testified that he didn't know why he was in this particular area, because he was supposed to go along an entirely different road to Holbrook. But he took another fork, for a reason he couldn't explain, and then he saw me. He said he felt guided. When they asked him how he got me down, he said he didn't know how he had been strong enough.

Like Lloyd, we are left to form our own opinions regarding the significance of Melburn's appearance. Some may choose to place more emphasis on the road patrolman's sense of being guided and strengthened than others. In any case, the imminence of deceased friends and relatives is obvious in this incident.

It appears that spirits not only feel our sorrows and joys, but they can take action to prevent tragedy. They are vital, living beings with powerful emotions. There is no hint of passive, dreamy floating away on a cloud in the wonder of the next world. The following is only one example of how they can take control of a situation.

> I was abandoned as a very small child. As a matter of fact, I was left in a movie theater when I was about five years old. From there, I was placed in the Southwest Children's Home in El Paso, Texas. I kicked around for a few years in and out of foster homes, about thirteen of them. Then I went to live with my real father's sister and my father's mother when I was twelve. After graduating from high school, I joined the Marine Corp in September, 1957.
>
> My grandmother passed away in 1958, while my grandfather had passed away about six months before that. Both were strong members of the Church, my grandfather having served many missions.
>
> I was at an army base where we were having joint military maneuvers with the army and the marines at Fort Smith, Arkansas. I had gone to sleep in an open barracks, but at about 1:00 a.m. I felt someone actually take me by the shoulder

and push on me. I woke up completely, sitting up in bed and putting my feet over the side. My grandmother was standing down at the bottom of my bunk, beside my footlocker. The first thing I thought of was that I should be frightened, but I was not.

I said, "Mimi," (that's what we all called her) "what are you doing here?"

She said, "I have something to tell you."

"What's that?"

"Your father is sick."

"My father, Gee, I haven't seen my dad for quite a few years. Where is he?"

She just said, very intensely, "Your father is sick." Then she turned around and walked away down the aisle.

I lay back down on my bunk and dozed off again. But in about five minutes I felt someone take me by both shoulders and shake me vigorously. I woke up and again put my feet out on the floor.

I said, "Mimi, what do you want?"

"Don't ignore me! I'm telling you your father is sick."

"I can't understand," I said. "I don't know what you are talking about."

Grandma Mimi was a spirited person in life, and she was really feisty now. "Don't you lay back down! Your father is sick." Then she turned around and just walked away again.

I sat there on the edge of my bunk and said to myself, *I have to be dreaming. This can't be.* But I got up and got dressed, and then I walked over to the commanding officer.

"I have to make a long distance phone call," I said.

"Okay, he shrugged. "There's the phone."

I called an aunt of mine who was one of Mimi's daughters. "Have you see my dad in the last little while?"

She said, "Why no, I haven't seen your dad in four or five years.

"Well, I have the strongest feeling something is wrong."

"What happened?" she asked.

"Mimi just came to me and shook me and said, 'Your father is sick.'"

My aunt started to cry. "Oh my h - - -," she said, "that is the same dream your Aunt Alice just had. She phoned me about thirty minutes ago."

"What are we going to do?"

"I don't know."

Then I asked, Has Mimi's house been sold?"

"No, we never sold the home. We had renters in it for a while, but right now it's vacant.

"Well, that's probably one of the first places you should go look."

"Yeah, she said. "I'll call you back."

I gave her the number, but it was the next morning before I heard from her. My father had gone to my grandmother's house and had gotten in through one of the back windows. He had had a heart attack, and my aunt found him on the floor nearly dead. He was taken to the hospital, and he lived.

Evidence is undeniable that the concern of deceased family members for loved ones reaches tangibly into the physical world. In the following experience, Orson F. Whitney, a member of the Quorum of the Twelve Apostles from 1906-1931, tells about a visit from his deceased wife and his conviction that she was acting in the capacity of a protector for him and his children:

> Early on the morning of April 24, 1918...while I lay on my pillow, half asleep, half awake, a pair of hands were laid upon my head. My first thought was that someone was in the house who ought not to be, and that I must lie perfectly still in order to be safe. But the touch was so soft and gentle that all fear left me, and with my own hands I took hold of those resting upon my head. They were a woman's hands. Presently I saw my wife Zina, who had been dead for eighteen years. She was hovering over me. It was all so real. I could not doubt that she was actually there, a guardian angel, watching over her children and me.[1]

We often take the idea of a guardian angel lightly, writing it off as a pet notion. However, Orson F. Whitney may have been entirely correct in designating his deceased wife as just such a being. There are so many accounts of guardian angels that it is impossible to dismiss the idea without consideration.

One interesting aspect common to accounts of guardian angels is how often this position is filled by deceased relatives. Several incidences of family members functioning protectively occurred early in

---

[1]Duane Crowther, *Life Everlasting*, p. 413. Crowther comments that previously Elder Whitney had received a blessing at the hands of Abraham O. Smoot promising that "If need be, thou shalt commune with the spirits that have gone hence, and they shall visit and revisit thee."

the afternoon on May 16, 1986, when David Young
and his wife went into the elementary school in
Cokeville, Wyoming, carrying a small arsenal of
weapons and pushing a cart containing a bomb. After herding 156 children and teachers into a classroom, they held them hostage. The afternoon wore
on, and then abruptly, there was a tremendous explosion that demolished the classroom. After the
explosion subsided, the bullets finished flying, and
the smoke cleared, nervous families found that the
Youngs had died alone. All the hostages had es-
caped alive. Bomb expert Richard Haskell observed
that "To say it was a miracle would be the under-
statement of the century."[2]

Many of the children have given simple explanations for their escape, and these startlingly attest
to help from the spirit world. Katrina and her sister
Rachel told their parents that some people spoke to
them that had not been in the room before. These
people came in through the ceiling and stood about
two feet off the floor:

> They were standing there above us...There
> was a mother and a father and a lady holding a
> tiny baby, and a little girl with long hair. There
> was a family of people. The woman told us the
> bomb was going off soon and to listen to our
> brother. He was going to come over and tell us
> what to do...
>
> She said to be sure we did what he told us. . . .

---

[2]Hartt and Judene Wixom, *Trial by Terror*, Bountiful, Ut.: Horizon Publishers
and Distributors, Inc., 1987, p. 144. Note: The following three quotes are a
re-cap of Wixom's findings as told in the same publication, *Trial by Terror*.

> They were all dressed in white, bright like a
> light bulb but brighter around the face...
>
> The woman made me feel good. I knew she
> loved me...She sort of smiled at me with her
> voice.

Katrina and Rachel's brother, Travis explained:

> I didn't see anyone, nothing!...I just heard a
> voice. It told me to find my little sisters and take
> them over by the window and keep them there. I
> did what I was told. I looked around and found
> them and told them to follow me over by the
> window...to stay there and not move...
>
> They were playing with their friends and I
> didn't think they would want to leave them. I
> knew they had to come with me. They got their
> coloring pages and I took them over by the win-
> dow...But I didn't stay there with them. I was also
> told to help them through the window when the
> bomb went off.

Katrina and Rachel's descriptions of the man as
looking familiar and the woman as having hair
like their mother eventually led the family to look
through old photos of living and deceased relatives.
Katrina picked up an old locket and said it looked
like the woman, except she didn't have glasses.
Rachel declared, "That's the angel! But without the
glasses." The woman in the picture was their
grandmother, who had died when their mother
was only sixteen.

All three children said that they had been praying for help when it came. Other hostages had similar experiences, and in most cases sincere prayers

preceded the spiritual messages or assistance given
to the hostages. No one seemed to be shocked or
frightened by the help they received.

Six-year-old Nathan said:

> A lady told me the bomb was going to go off
> very soon. She told me how to save myself. She
> said to go over by the window, then hurry out
> when I heard the bomb explode. She told me that
> I would make it if I did exactly what she said.

Nathan had never seen the lady before, but, like
Katrina and Rachel, he later identified the person
in a photo. She was his deceased great-grand-
mother.

No one knew when the bomb would explode, or
even that it would. Yet several children were told
that it "would happen shortly." Katrina, Rachel,
Travis and Nathan's experiences, among others,
happened without any previous discussion of angels or supernatural help. The children spoke of it
"independently, not after discussion among themselves."[3]

The concern of deceased family members for
those left behind in mortality suggests that loved
ones hold a place in the uppermost thoughts of
spirits. Their preoccupation with loved ones implies that family is of great importance throughout
the eternal plan of our Father. Because of this, encounters with the spirit world would invariably

---

[3]Hartt and Judene Wixom, *Trial by Terror*, pp. 150-160.

lead us to reflect on the significance families should hold in mortality.

While Church callings and other obligations extend for a limited time, the responsibilities of parenthood are eternal. If we are to preserve the blessings of family ties throughout the eternities, Boyd K. Packer has counseled us that in mortality, "everything must be done to see that there is something worthy of preserving."[4]

---

[4]Boyd K. Packer, Address given at genealogical seminar, Aug. 6, 1970.

Questions and Answers

1. Under what circumstances may a spirit visit the mortal world?

It appears that on special occasions a departed spirit may visit a mortal being to provide comfort, give instruction, or rescue someone from imminent death or tragedy.

We have read in this chapter about Orson F. Whitney receiving comfort from the presence of his departed wife, and a few of the cases where protective guidance was received by children during a hostage-crisis. It is possible that Melburn Archibald, who had died only two days previously, intervened to prevent the untimely death of his friend, Lloyd. Likewise, it is certain that Mimi was permitted to warn her grandson and daughter of the serious condition of her son, whose death was avoided because of her visits. President Joseph F. Smith said of spirits' visiting privileges:

> Our fathers and mothers, brothers, sisters, and friends who have passed away from this earth, having been faithful and worthy to enjoy these rights and privileges, may have a mission given them to visit their relatives and friends upon the earth again, bringing from the Divine Presence messages of love, of warning of reproof and in-

struction to those whom they had learned to love in the flesh.[5]

According to Parley P. Pratt, these spirits are not free to wander or move about unless they are assigned to do so, although spirits influenced by Satan may haunt the earth and create whatever evil or mischief they choose.[6]

There are many examples of mortals who have had involvement with spirit beings, usually to give comfort. It is less common for loved ones to come in answer to a fervent prayer, yet during his imprisonment, Parley P. Pratt cried to the Lord to know if he would ever be delivered. His departed wife gave him the answer.

A personage from the world of spirits stood before me with a smile of compassion in every look, and pity mingled with tenderest love and sympathy in every expression of the countenance. A soft hand seemed placed within my own, and a glowing cheek was laid in tenderness and warmth upon mine. A well-known voice saluted me, which I readily recognized as that of the wife of my youth...I was made to realize that she was sent to commune with me, and answer my question...Knowing this, I said to her in a most earnest and inquiring tone, 'Shall I ever be at liberty again in this life and enjoy the society of my family and the saints, and preach the Gospel

---

[5]Smith, *Gospel Doctrine*, pp. 435-436.

[6]Pratt, *Key to Science of Theology*, p. 110.

as I have done?' She answered definitely and un-
hesitatingly, 'YES!'[7]

Lorenzo Dow Young's experience is an excellent
example of a spirit acting as a guide:

> In a moment, I was out of the body, and fully
> conscious that I had made the change. At once, a
> heavenly messenger, or guide was by me...I was
> under the control of the man [and]...I begged of
> him the privilege of speaking to [my family] but
> he said he could not grant it.[8]

David P. Kimball's mother and father appeared
to him while he was lost in the Arizona desert and
provided the help that saved his life:

> While in this terrible plight, and when I had
> just about given up all hope, my father and
> mother appeared to me and gave me a drink of
> water and comforted me, telling me I would be
> found by my friends who were out searching for
> me, and that I would live two years longer as I
> had been promised.[9]

Another reason for visitations is to give someone important information about the work of the

---

[7] Parley P. Pratt, *Autobiography of Parley P. Pratt*, 6th ed., Salt Lake City, Ut.: Deseret Book Co., 1966, pp. 238-239.

[8] Lorenzo Dow Young, "Lorenzo Dow Young's Narrative," *Fragments of Experience*, (Sixth Book of the Faith-Promoting series), Salt Lake City: Juvenile Instructor's Office, 1882, pp. 27-28.

[9] Orson F. Whitney, *Helpful Visions*, p. 14. Like the story about Mimi, this is an example of a supernatural rescue, one of the elements added to the 'Death Model' in Dr. Moody's book, *Reflections of Life After Life*.

kingdom. Wilford Woodruff said he had an interview with the Prophet Joseph Smith in the spirit world. He said that many things were laid before him during the interview, but that when he awoke, they were taken from him, and he could not comprehend them.[10]

Other spirit-mortal involvements seem to be related to guardian angels. John Peterson described the personage that guided him through a death experience in these words:

> It was between ten and eleven o'clock that a visitor suddenly made his appearance in the room, and standing by the couch on which I lay, placed his hand on my head and asked if I were ready to go? I answered, "Yes," and just at that instant I seemed to stand upon the floor, my body lying on the bed. I looked around to see if my father could see us, but he seemed too interested in reading to have noticed us. We started off on our journey through space, seemingly with the rapidity of lightning (for I can make no other comparison). I asked my guide who he was. He answered that he was one of the guardian angels sent to bring the dead.[11]

There is not sufficient evidence to conclude that everyone is watched over by a guardian angel at every moment. On the other hand, sometimes

---

[10]Wilford Woodruff, *Journal of Discourses*, 3:227-30. This corresponds with the 'Vision of Knowledge,' another element added to Moody's model in *Reflections on Life After Life*.

[11]John Peterson, "Was Dead and Came to Life Again," *Millennial Star*, Vol. 68, 1916, p. 699.

more than one heavenly messenger has been sent
to deliver the Lord's servants from the clutches of
Satan or from other danger. Wilford Woodruff reported that as a missionary three beings delivered
him and his companion from evil.[12]

We also cannot assume that all spirits are assigned to watch over mortals. Some are assigned to
other tasks and are not constantly aware of the actions of their mortal loved ones.[13]

2. *Why is it that some mortals have experiences*
   with departed spirits, but others do not?

One answer to this question could be related to
spiritual gifts.[14] One of these gifts is "the discerning
of spirits," and, like the other gifts, is not given to
skeptics either in or out of the church. People who
have had such experiences have generally prepared
for them. For example, Joseph F. Smith had been
reading and pondering on the writings of Peter and
the Lord's visit to the spirit world, as well as the
atoning sacrifice of the Savior. In that spirit of pondering and reflecting, he explained that, "The eyes
of my understanding were opened, and the Spirit of
the Lord rested upon me, and I saw the hosts of the
dead, both small and great...." (D&C 138:11)

However, there are occasions where a situation
exists where the spirit messenger must work
through anyone that can be reached.

---

[12]Wilford Woodruff, *Journal of Discourses*, Vol. 4, p. 2.

[13]"Manifestation About Building Temples," *Deseret Evening News*, May 18,
     1918. Also note Heber Q. Hale's comments regarding this in the Epilogue.

[14]See I Cor. 12:1-12, Moroni 10:8-17, and D&C 46:13-29.

Last, we must remember that such encounters with the righteous dead cannot be summoned at will. President Brigham Young warned:

> (Evil spirits) are visiting the human family with various manifestations... Always look for an opposite power, an evil power, to give manifestations also: look out for the counterfeit... Are there any communications from evil spirits? Yes; and the devil is making the people believe very strongly in revelations from the spirit world.

3. Do habits and inclinations differ in mortality and the spirit world?

Elder Bruce R. McConkie concisely answered this question:

> Life and work and activity all continue in the spirit world. Men have the same talents and intelligence there which they had in this life. They possess the same attitudes, inclinations, and feelings there which they had in this life. They believe the same things, as far as eternal truths are concerned; they continue to walk in the same path they were following in this life. Amulek said "that same spirit which doth possess your bodies at the time that ye go out of this life...will have power to possess your body in that eternal world."[15]

---

[15]Alma 34:34, Bruce R. McConkie, *Mormon Doctrine*, p. 762. Heber C. Kimball also said that he had been on the other side of the veil in a vision and had seen rebellious spirits still fighting against God and His servants.

In spite of this, there is a chance for change in the spirit world. Melvin J. Ballard said:

> It is my judgment that any man or woman can do more to conform to the laws of God in one year in this life than they could in ten years when they are dead. The spirit can repent and change, and then the battle has to go forward with the flesh afterwards. It is much easier to overcome and serve the Lord when both flesh and spirit are combined as one... We will find when we are dead every desire, every feeling will be greatly intensified... It will take them a thousand years to do what it would have taken but three score years to accomplish in this life.[16]

George Ritchie reported seeing people, unaware of spirit beings right beside them, talking, trying to communicate, but having no success. He described spirit beings grasping for cigarettes and liquor glasses, but unable to grip them. These people, he concluded had set their hearts on worldly pleasures and after death their inclinations continued to chain them to earthly substance, power, and recognition.[17]

Clearly, the spirit world is an extension of mortality and the changes a person faces there are a new location and separation from his body.

---

[16]Melvin J. Ballard, *"Three Degrees of Glory-A Discourse,"* Salt Lake City, Ut.: Magazine Printing Co., 1955, pp. 46-47.

[17]Ritchie, *Return From Tomorrow*, pp. 56-61.

4. What is it like to be without a body?

The answer to this question is well documented. Brigham Young said that in the spirit world, everything will appear as natural as things do now. Spirits will communicate as freely there as they do here in their bodies, but there will be freedom from pain and distress.[18]

Many experiences document relief from pain, as well as pointing to ease of movement. On 3 February 1887, the night following his death, Briant Stevens appeared to his father in a dream. His father said that Briant's spirit-body moved about almost without effort. In fact, simply by inclining his head, he could project his body in any direction he wanted to go.[19] Brigham Young taught:

> (Once our spirits are unlocked from our bodies, they can) move with ease and lightning. If we want to visit Jerusalem, or this, that, or the other place — and I presume we will be permitted if we desire — there we are looking at its streets... If we wish to understand how they are living here on these western islands, or in China, we are there; in fact, we are like the light of the morning, or I will not say the electric fluid, but its operations on the wires... If we want to behold Jerusalem as it was in the days of the Savior; or if we want to see the Garden of Eden as it was when it was created, there we are. . . .[20]

---

[18]Brigham Young, *Journal of Discourses*, Vol. 14, p. 231.

[19]Kenyon, (comp.), *Helpful Visions*, Salt Lake City, Ut.: Juvenile Instructor's Office, 1887, p. 36.

[20]Brigham Young, *Journal of Discourses*, Vol. 14, p. 231.

Orson Pratt taught that our bodies seem to limit us in some ways by comparing the body to the scaffolding around a building, which is used to work on the building. He indicated that there would be other ways of gaining knowledge as spirits than through reliance only on our senses.

We need not suppose our five senses connect us with all the things of heaven, and earth, and eternity, and space... Suppose He should give us a sixth sense, a seventh, an eighth, a ninth, or a fiftieth. All these different senses would convey to us new ideas, as much as the senses of tasting, smelling, or seeing communicate different ideas from that of hearing... There is a faculty mentioned...which we are not in possession of here...that is not only to see a vast number of things in the same moment, looking in all directions by the aid of the spirit, but also to obtain a vast number of ideas at the same instant...knowledge will rush in from all quarters; it will come in like the light which flows from the sun, penetrating every part. . . .[21]

Although there is an expansion of the senses and the power of perception in the spirit world, we should remember:

---

[21]Orson Pratt, *Journal of Discourses*, Vol. 2, pp. 230, 244-245, 247. Some of Dr. Moody's subjects glimpsed an entire separate realm of existence in which all knowledge, past, present, future appeared to exist in a timeless state. *Reflections on Life After Life*, pp. 9-14.

> For man is spirit. The elements are eternal,
> and spirit and element, inseparably connected,
> receive a fulness of joy. (D&C 93:33)

In D&C 45:17, the Lord states that the dead had looked upon the long absence from their bodies as a bondage. Therefore, in spite of his expanded spiritual perception, man cannot receive a fullness of joy until his spirit and body are again reunited in the resurrection. This is because spirit and body together make up the soul of man.

5. Are spirits tangible to mortals?

In section 129 of the Doctrine and Covenants, Joseph Smith instructs that "There are two kinds of beings in heaven, namely: Angels, who are resurrected personages, having bodies of flesh and bones; Secondly: the spirits of just men made perfect, they who are not resurrected, but inherit the same glory." (vs. 1,3) He explains, "If he be an angel he will do so [shake hands with you] and you will feel his hand." (vs. 5) However, "If he be the spirit of a just man made perfect he will come in his glory; for that is the only way he can appear." (vs. 6)

Because some of the experiences in this chapter (Mimi shaking her grandson by the shoulders and Orson Whitney's physical contact with his wife) describe touching and feeling spirits, we must assume in light of D&C 129 that their experiences were either out-of-the-body or that they were communicating with resurrected beings. One of these conditions seems to fit most cases.[22] For example, President Joseph F. Smith gave the following account of his experience with individuals who had all passed away.

> I knocked and the door opened, and the man who stood there was the Prophet Joseph Smith... He clasped my hand and drew me in, then closed the great door. I felt his hand just as tangibly as I ever felt the hand of a man. I knew him, and when I entered I saw my father, and Brigham, and Heber, and Willard, and other good men that I had known standing in a row... My mother was there, and she sat with a child in her lap... I went to my mother and picked up the child and thought it was a fine baby boy. I carried it to the Prophet, and as I handed it to him I purposely thrust my hands up against his breast. I felt the warmth... Now, I suppose that this is only a dream? To me it is a reality. There never could be anything more real to me. I felt the hand of Joseph Smith.[23]

6. Do personality, individuality, or recognizability change with death?

Considering the experiences already presented and Elder Bruce R. McConkie and Elder Melvin J. Ballard's statements that habits and inclinations are not changed by death, we can presume that indi-

---

[22]There is no indication that the instruction in D&C 129 was meant to apply to contact between spirits. In fact, there is ample evidence to the contrary, as addressed in question #7.

[23]Joseph F. Smith, *Gospel Doctrine*, pp. 542-543.

viduality does not change with death. Erastus Snow asked:

> How does Brother Snow's spirit look when it is disembodied? Why, you just look at me now, and you can answer the question. How does the spirit of my wife look? Why, just look at her and see. And if we are disembodied at the same instant, we should scarcely know that we were changed any more than we would if we both started out the door at the same instant and found ourselves outside, looking at each other . . . .[24]

We know that our appearance is identical after death because the Savior told the brother of Jared that the spirit and body look alike:

> Behold, this body, which ye now behold, is the body of my spirit; and man have I created after the body of my spirit; and even as I appear unto thee to be in the spirit will I appear unto my people in the flesh. (Ether 3:16)

Such continuity is only logical, and even without the wealth of revelation that we currently enjoy, men have borne witness to the truth of this idea.

---

[24]Erastus Snow, *Journal of Discourses*, Vol. 19, pp. 273-274.

7. *What evidence is there that spirits are tangible
to other spirits?*

In the Doctrine and Covenants Section 131: 7-8
we read:

> There is no such thing as immaterial matter.
> All spirit is matter, but it is more fine or pure,
> and can only be discerned by purer eyes;
> We cannot see it; but when our bodies are
> purified we shall see that it is all matter.

Joseph Smith taught that the spirits of the dead
are in a place where they can converse as they did
on earth.[25] Brigham Young added:

> Spirits are just as familiar with spirits as bod-
> ies are with bodies, though spirits are composed
> of matter so refined as not to be tangible to this
> coarser organization. They walk, converse, and
> have their meetings.[26]

8. *To what extent do spirits interact with resurrected beings?*

The Prophet Joseph Smith explained:

---

[25]Joseph Smith, *History of the Church*, Vol. 6, p. 311.

[26]Brigham Young, *Journal of Discourses*, Vol. 3, pp. 371-372. Parley P. Pratt
said: "The elements and beings in the spirit world are as real and tangible to
spirit organs as things and beings of the temporal world are to beings of a
temporal state." Pratt, *Key to Science of Theology*, p. 126.

Flesh and bones cannot go there [the spirit world]; but flesh and bones, quickened by the spirit of God, can.[27]

This tells us that resurrected personages can visit the world of spirits. President Brigham Young indicated that interactions between resurrected beings and disembodied spirits are one-way affairs:

We will take the best men we can find — when they pass through the veil they are in happiness, they are in glory, they go among the disembodied spirits; but they do not go where there are resurrected bodies, for they cannot live there. A Prophet or an Apostle cannot live there. They also go into the spiritual world to live with spirits. Do they commune with the Father and Son? The Father communes with them as He pleases, through the means of angels, or otherwise the Son and the Holy Ghost. This is the situation of the Prophet, the Apostle, and all the saints before they receive their resurrected bodies. . . .[28]

From this we can see that whatever interaction takes place between spirits and resurrected beings is carefully controlled and cannot be initiated by the spirit being.

---

[27]Joseph Smith, *History of the Church*, Vol. 6, p. 52.

[28]Brigham Young, *Journal of Discourses*, Vol. 6, pp. 293-294.

SECTION III

Spirit World Environment

4

Preliminary Judgment

One common element among many out-of-the-body and near death experiences is a panoramic, instantaneous preliminary judgment. Those who have witnessed this do not describe it as a scene of condemnation, but as a review of life that is overwhelming in its dimensions.

George Albert Smith's experience is often spoken of and is known by primary children as the 'what have you done with my name?' story. Because it is so well known, it provides a familiar and easy to understand description of the judgment experience.

> A number of years ago I was seriously ill; in fact, I think everyone gave me up but my wife...
> One day under these conditions, I lost consciousness of my surroundings and thought I had passed to the Other Side. I found myself standing

with my back to a large and beautiful lake, facing
a great forest of trees. There was no one in sight,
and there was no boat upon the lake or any other
visible means to indicate how I might have arrived there. I realized, or seemed to realize, that I
had finished my work in mortality and had gone
home. I began to look around, to see if I could not
find someone. There was no evidence of anyone
living there, just those great, beautiful trees in
front of me and the wonderful lake behind me.

I began to explore, and soon I found a trail
through the woods which seemed to have been
used very little, and which was almost obscured
by grass. I followed this trail, and after I had
walked for some time and traveled a considerable
distance through the forest, I saw a man coming
towards me.

I hurried my steps to reach him because I
recognized him as my grandfather. In mortality
he weighed over three hundred pounds, so you
may know he was a large man. I remember how
happy I was to see him coming. I had been given
his name and had always been proud of it.

When Grandfather came within a few feet of
me, he stopped. His stopping was an invitation
for me to stop. Then — and this I would like the
boys and girls and young people never to forget
— he looked at me very earnestly and said,

"I would like to know what you have done
with my name."

Everything I had ever done passed before me
as though it were a flying picture on a screen —
everything I had done. Quickly this vivid retro-
spect came down to the very time I was standing
there. My whole life passed before me. I smiled
and looked at my grandfather and said,

"I have never done anything with your name
of which you need be ashamed."

He stepped forward and took me in his
arms...[1]

From the foregoing account, President George
Albert Smith described seeing every detail of his life
as if it were a flying picture on a screen.

In the following story, we find a very similar account:

When I am pregnant, I have a hormone im-
balance that affects my entire glandular system.
Although I have sought the best medical advice
available, when I am expecting I become seriously
ill, and have lost nine out of my eleven pregnancies.

During one of these pregnancies, I became so
weak and tired that I could not walk across the
room to call on the phone for help. I was having
very heavy contractions and knew that I was not
going to make it through that pregnancy. But I
also knew that my own life was endangered, and
I prayed to Heavenly Father that someone would
come to help me. As I lay for hours in this condition, I began to ponder the events of my life. I
thought about some of the things I had done that
I liked and others that I did not. Suddenly I began
to pray with fervent desire that I might know
how I stood with the Lord. I had tried all my life
to repent. Had I been forgiven?

---

[1]Preston Nibley, *Sharing the Gospel With Others*, Salt Lake City, Ut.: Deseret
Book Co., 1948, pp. 111-112.

In an instant, my position changed. Although
I was lying upon my bed, I was also seeing a play
before me on stage that looked like the book of
life, and I was the main character. In it, I saw
some things for which I felt sorry. I had been
seeking forgiveness, and seeing these things
made me ask the Lord more fervently, "Hast
Thou truly forgiven me of this?" Then a huge
page of the book-of-life came right over the top of
the scene I was worried about and I heard the
words, *"Thy sins are forgiven thee; remember
them no more."*

Only a few moments later, my husband came
in to check on me. I was unspeakably relieved
that he had come home, and as I tried to ask him
for help, I started to miscarry. The physical labor
was too much for my body because of my weak-
ened condition. My body stayed right there, but
my spirit started leaving. My husband began
slapping my face, yet I couldn't respond. I knew
that I was passing on, and I watched myself leaving.

Suddenly I started going through dimensions.
There is no way to describe what happened. I was
moving through our physical dimension into
another one. The dimension did not stay in one
shape or size, and I was aware that I was moving
through circles and triangles and squares toward
a bright light. I was so taken in by the sizes of
things that I don't remember any colors.

Before I reached the light, I recalled my life in
a sudden flash. It was the most totally exciting,
fantastic thing I have ever seen. I saw the time I
was brought from heaven to the earth by angels
to a body, how I was received at the hospital, and
how my parents loved me. From that day until

the present, I saw everything that ever happened to me in my life. It was all in an instant, at fantastic speeds and rates, and it was not like a day-by-day procedure. What I saw was like a concept to learn or a trial, experience by experience. My life was arranged systematically so that everything related to one subject or trial was grouped together. At the end of each experience I was judged. There was no voice of judgment, but I knew instantly how the Lord felt about each thing I had done in my life. I was also able to perceive how my actions affected everyone around me. I had never even thought about my influence on others as part of my judgment before, only what I had done.

The entire experience is almost overwhelming, but it was not too much for me because my mind was capable of great acceleration. I could comprehend many things quickly and vividly. It is impossible to explain. Here, we are just like turtles — everything we do is *so slow*. I had instant recall about every incident I was ever involved in, as if I were living my life again in its entirety, but I was understanding it this time, and how it affected others.

For example, my brother wasn't even a year older than I was. As a child I could not understand why he would beat me up and not treat me like a best friend. From this experience, I learned that he disliked being physically smaller than I was. Everyone treated us like I was older because I grew faster. I had never thought of this until that moment. Then I knew how he felt, and what's more, I knew how I could have helped him. I was deeply disappointed that I had not understood his anxiety.

This realization bothered me and, as I sorrowed over the breach in my relationship with my brother, I was told I would not be judged on what I did not know. I was to be judged on what I did know in life and on what I would have done had I known more. I knew in that instant what I would have done if I had possessed more knowledge and the judgment on that as well as on my actions. I was told that this experience had been one of his trials. My brother had already died, and I asked how he was doing and how he perceived this. I was given the knowledge that he had already had the same experience and that he was very happy in the spirit world.

The most wonderful part of this experience was that all the things I had done wrong were gone as if they had never existed. For the first time, I truly understood the beauty of the Atonement. If I had not just had the experience of having my sins forgiven, this would still have been glorious beyond description, but guilt and sorrow would have weighed my soul down with pain.

Instead, I was filled with supreme joy. There were things I had forgotten about entirely that I was able to enjoy again in the fullest sense. I felt the sweetest joy in realizing that trials really do stack up like stairs, the way we are taught in church. Each trial prepares you for the next one, bringing you a blessing of knowledge or wisdom or experience. A sudden, inspiring recognition of how carefully our own individual tests are planned burst over me, and I was filled with gratitude.

I will never be afraid of death. I want to experience the exhilaration of that judgment scene again, the feeling of God's love and compassion sweeping through me. It was awesome — in the true meaning of the word. As the review ended, I was given my judgment. I knew exactly how I stood, and I was very pleased with it and its fairness.

I experienced this judgment as I was nearing the bright light. Then I saw someone coming toward me, with many other people behind him. He was an angel who had come to get me. I don't know who he was, but he was someone who had always helped me. We had been familiar with one another for a very long time, and it would have been ridiculous to make an introduction at this point. I was excited and wanted to express my happiness at the relief I felt from the cares of the world, but I was told that I had made some promises and commitments and had been set apart to do some work before this world was. I had accepted a responsibility that would have a great missionary effect.

I was shown another child that I would have if I returned, but I was also shown what would happen to my children if I did not. I was given the choice and knew that either way, all would go well. At that moment, I was most caught up in the fact that I had made a commitment that I had not even begun to fulfill.

As I marvelled on how this work was to be done, I was shown that the Savior was in charge of the work, and that He would lead me. It was clear that the Lord would provide everything that would be necessary for the work.

Then, I knew that I had to choose at that instant or my physical body would be too far gone. I was asked to return, but at the same time I was promised a complete reward for what I had done if I remained. At that moment, I made a full oath and commitment to do the work that the Lord had for me to do. It is my witness that everything necessary to the work has been provided, and I have been sustained in every situation.

As soon as I chose to return, my ability to communicate vanished. I shot back through the dimensions and was aware of my husband still slapping my face.

Returning was an awful thing. There was incredible anguish in coming back to the imperfections, sorrows, and pains of this world. I felt great sadness and a sense of incompleteness as my abilities were again limited. No longer could I know other's thoughts as they pertained to me in the complete way I had experienced. Everything felt slow in this 'turtle' world.

My husband rushed me to the hospital where I was hooked up to a lot of machinery. They said that I was beyond medical help. My temperature was ten degrees low, and didn't rise to a normal level for days. My pulse was gone. However, my mind was keen, and I had the ability to communicate. Over time I have recovered and had that last child, but it did not happen right away. My recovery took years.

My experience did not leave me unchanged. I have enjoyed a quickening of my abilities. I can read, think, and comprehend things four times as fast as I could before. My perceptions of others and the 'entire scope' of things has broadened, my spiritual and intellectual abilities have been increased, and I can perceive the degree of light or darkness within individuals that I meet.[2] Above all, I have a heightened awareness of the value of the Atonement, repentance, and the plan of salvation. The only way we can be saved from total, devastating hell is through Christ. My love for the Savior is virtually impossible to put into words. I am entirely committed to serving Him.

---

[2]Jedediah M. Grant had a similar ability after his visit to the spirit world. See Chapter 5.

Questions and Answers

1. What is the review or judgment like? How extensive are our recollections, regrets, and joys?

The scriptural basis for our Christian belief in a judgment is well-documented. Here is one Biblical reference:

> And I saw the dead, small and great, stand before God; and the books were opened: and another book was opened, which is the book of life: and the dead were judged out of those things which were written in the books, according to their works. (Revelation 20:12)

Latter-day revelation also supports the validity of a judgment:

> For I, the Lord, will judge all men according to their works, according to the desire of their hearts. (D&C 137:9)

These scriptures refer to a judgment that is related to the resurrection. However, there is firm scriptural and experiential evidence that a preliminary judgment occurs at the time of death, involving a review of a person's life and an assignment to a specific place in the spirit world. The prophet Alma understood this principle well and taught it to his wayward son, Corianton.

Now, concerning the state of the soul between death and the resurrection — Behold, it has been made known unto me by an angel, that the spirits of all men, as soon as they are departed from this mortal body...are taken home to that God who gave them life.

And then shall it come to pass, that the spirits of those who are righteous are received into a state of happiness, which is called paradise, a state of rest, a state of peace, where they shall rest from all their troubles and from all care, and sorrow.

And...the spirits of the wicked...shall be cast out into outer darkness. (Alma 40:11-13)

In both of this chapter's experiences, the teller explained that he reviewed his own life instantaneously and knew for himself what his judgment would be. Interestingly, Dr. Moody found this type of a review to be very common in his study, and described it as an 'incredibly vivid' display of visual imagery.[3]

2. *Do spirits have a recollection of pre-earth life after death?*

In spite of all the evidence for a judgment or review following death, we have found no authoritative source indicating that there is also a review of anyone's pre-earthly activities. Joseph Smith taught:

When you climb a ladder, you must begin at the bottom, and ascend step by step, until you ar-

---

[3]Moody, *Life After Life*, pp. 64-73.

rive at the top; and so it is with the principles of the Gospel — you must begin with the first, and go on until you learn all the principles of exaltation. But it will be a great while after you have passed through the veil before you have learned them. It is not all to be comprehended in this world; it will be a great work to learn our salvation and exaltation even beyond the grave.[4]

It seems that if we were to have the veil removed from our memory of the pre-earth life our agency would be curtailed, and we know that men continue to enjoy their free agency in the spirit world. Yet, we may suppose that the final judgment associated with the resurrection will have to consider the pre-earth life if it is to be complete. In any case, we know that we become the sum total of our thoughts, feelings, and actions. These shape the character of our spirits, whether they have occurred in the pre-earth life, mortality, or the spirit world.

3. Are all departed spirits in the same location? Where are they?

In order to understand what happens to the spirit at death, we must consider the words of President Joseph Fielding Smith, who cautioned that the phrase "taken home to God," simply means that their mortal existence has come to an end, and they have returned to the world of spirits.

Brigham Young taught:

---

[4]Joseph Fielding Smith, *Teachings of the Prophet Joseph Smith.* Salt Lake City, Ut.: The Deseret News Press, 1938, p. 348.

Where is the spirit world? It is right here. Do
the good and evil spirits go together? Yes, they
do. Do they both inhabit one kingdom? yes, they
do... Do they go beyond the boundaries of this
organized earth? No, they do not. They are
brought forth upon this earth, for the express
purpose of inhabiting it to all eternity. Where
else are you going? Nowhere else, only as you
may be permitted.[5]

Upon arrival in the next world, spirits are assigned a place according to their works.[6] However,
within that world there are two major divisions:
Paradise, where the righteous dwell, and spirit
prison for the wicked. Until the death of Christ,
these two divisions were separated by a great gulf,
with no exchange between them. However, after
the Savior visited the spirit world, the gulf between
them was bridged and the righteous began teaching
the gospel to the wicked. When the wicked spirits
repent, they leave their prison hell and join the
righteous in paradise.[7]

The nature of hell was described by the Prophet
Joseph Smith when he explained that the great

---

[5]Brigham Young, *Journal of Discourses*, Vol. 3, p. 369. Parley P. Pratt further
commented: ". . .the earth and other planets of a like sphere, have their
inward or spiritual spheres, as well as their outward, or temporal. The one
is peopled by temporal tabernacles, and the other by spirits. A veil is
drawn between the one sphere and the other, whereby all the objects in the
spiritual sphere are rendered invisible to those in the temporal. Pratt, *Key
to the Science of Theology*, pp. 126-127.

[6]Joseph Fielding Smith, *Answers to Gospel Questions*. Salt Lake City, Ut.:
Deseret Book Co., 1959, Vol. 2, p. 85.

[7]Bruce R. McConkie, *Mormon Doctrine*, p. 762. See also the "Vision of the
Redemption of the Dead" in D&C 138:11-30.

misery of departed spirits is to know that they have fallen short of the glory they could have had if they had obeyed the gospel.[8]

George Ritchie described just such anguish when he recounted having witnessed scenes of 'spirits imprisoned or enslaved' by their own earthly habits. He described the living people as being surrounded by a luminous glow, and others (spirits) without the glow were trying unsuccessfully to communicate with them. Some spirits were so chained to their earthly habits, that he wondered if hell meant remaining where the spirit's desires were, in the physical realm of earth, but never again being able to make physical contact with it. He saw people fighting each other, but making no physical contact. They were kicking, fighting, and pantomiming abuses and perversions he had never dreamed of. The entire worldly plane was protected by beings of light who were attending, watching over, and ministering to the others.[9]

Based on these sources, we can see that although the spirit world is on this earth, it is in a different dimension, with two major divisions — Paradise for the righteous, and Spirit Prison for the wicked.

4. *What about suicide? Are there serious consequences?*

Elder Bruce R. McConkie defined suicide as "the voluntary and intentional taking of one's own life, particularly where the person involved is account-

---

[8]Smith, *Teachings of the Prophet Joseph Smith*, p. 310.

[9]Ritchie, *Return From Tomorrow*, p. 63-66.

able and has a sound mind."[10] Four key words qualify this definition and show us that suicide is an act that is voluntary, intentional, and must be done by someone who is accountable. Because of this, suicide may not be an appropriate term for describing some instances where individuals take their own lives while in a state of severe depression or under the influence of drugs.

Although the scriptures are silent on the subject of suicide, it has nevertheless been condemned by prophets of this dispensation. An official letter from the First Presidency said:

> Suicide should be made odious among the people of God, it should be emphasized as a deadly sin, and no undue feelings of tenderness toward the unfortunate dead, or of sympathy towards the living bereaved, should prevent us denouncing it as a crime against God and humanity, against the Creator and the creature. It is true that the exact enormity of the act is not defined with minute detail in the Holy Scriptures, or the limits of its punishment given; but to believers of the God whom we worship it has always been regarded as a sin of great magnitude...[11]

---

[10] McConkie, *Mormon Doctrine*, p. 771.

[11] James R. Clark, *Messages of the First Presidency*. Salt Lake City, Ut.: Bookcraft, Inc., 1965., Vol. 3, p. 88.

President Spencer W. Kimball not only taught that suicide was wrong, but that anything we intentionally do to shorten life is sinful.[12]

About the condition of those who take their own life, he said,

> ...To commit suicide is a sin if one is normal in his thinking. We should avoid becoming disturbed in our minds or thinking about it... So if the party is mentally well, he has the responsibility to keep himself well and his thinking clear...No one in his 'right mind,' and especially if he has an understanding of the gospel, will permit himself to arrive at this "point of no return."[13]
>
> Sometimes the temptation toward suicide comes when a person is bowed in grief at bereavement or feeling inadequate to meet and cope with the difficult situations he encounters. To end it all! But this great crime does not end it. In his right mind, only a fool would ever consider taking his own life.[14]

While the attitude we should take toward personal thoughts of suicide or the taking of one's own life is clear, Elder Bruce R. McConkie cautioned us not to judge those who take away their own lives:

---

[12]Edward L. Kimball, *ed., The Teachings of Spencer W. Kimball.* Salt Lake City, Ut.: Bookcraft, Inc., 1982, p. 187.

[13]Kimball, *The Teachings of Spencer W. Kimball,* pp. 187-188.

[14]Spencer W. Kimball, *The Miracle of Forgiveness.* Salt Lake City, Ut.: Bookcraft Inc., 1969, p. 130.

No man has the right to run away from these tests, no matter how severe they may be, by taking his own life. Obviously persons subject to great stresses may lose control of themselves and become mentally clouded to the point that they are no longer accountable for their acts. Such are not to be condemned for taking their own lives. It should also be remembered that judgment is the Lord's; He knows the thoughts, intents, and abilities of men; and He in His infinite wisdom will make all things right in due course.[15]

Lest anyone might ignore the warnings of the prophets about the seriousness of suicide, we will also mention that Dr. Moody found near-death experiences with suicide to be uniformly unpleasant. He quotes one woman as saying: "If you leave here a tormented soul, you will be a tormented soul over there, too."[16] In short, they report that the conflicts they were trying to escape through suicide were still present when they died, but with added complications. The fact that death does not erase problems leads again to George Ritchie's description of the realm of bewildered spirits. If we are tied to earthly things, death will only separate us from them physically.

---

[15]McConkie, *Mormon Doctrine*, p. 771.

[16]Moody, *Life After Life*, p. 143.

5

A Beautiful World

No matter who tells the experience, nor what their background is, one unchanging element in all accounts of the spirit world environment is that it is beautiful beyond description. The following story may sound a bit fantastical to our general, worldly conceptions, but its elements are in agreement with the experiences of many individuals, published and otherwise:

> Late in 1978, when I was about nine going on ten, our family's puppy was killed in a car accident. At first we hoped Poky would survive, and I put every ounce of love I had into believing that he would make it, but he didn't. My heart was broken. I wanted to know where the animals go after they die. My mother said she had not thought about it before, but my brothers and I kept after her for an answer. It was the uppermost

thing in my mind and prayers for days, until one night when I had a dream.

I was asleep when I heard a voice that called me by name,

"Jose, follow me."

I did not see anyone, but I followed the voice through a tunnel. When I came out of it there was a giant fifty-foot gate of gold that opened when I got near it. By the gate was Poky, our puppy.

Poky did not bark in his usual way, but spoke to me through my mind. I knew his thoughts, but he did not speak them like the voice I had followed.

I went inside the gate with him and saw a nice road, built of golden bricks. There was a beautiful field with flowers and trees, and nearby were some pleasant houses like cottages. A woman in a white dress came out of a house and walked down the road. She greeted me, telling me that she was my grandmother who had died when I was very young. I can't remember what else she said, but we spoke for a minute and then she went her way.

After that I followed Poky through the field and I was surprised that the flowers did not die when I stepped on them. I saw other animals as well, a lion and a monkey.

Then Poky made it clear that I had to go and he led me to the gate. There was no good-bye, just a knowledge that I had to go, and then I woke up. In the years since this dream, I have asked myself if this is just the fantasy of a small boy, but I do not believe so. Some of the things were different than I ever would have imagined, and I do not feel inside that it was a dream. Neither did my mother.

Generally, we would not expect a little boy to dream about a field of flowers, so it is interesting to note that both Jose and Rodney noticed beautiful flowers. In the following dream, Carma also describes extraordinarily beautiful plants and buildings equally impressive as the fifty-foot golden gates in Jose's dream:

My mother died when I was nine and a half years old, and although I had a very happy teenage time, I often missed her terribly. I planned the kind of marriage I wanted and was content with it, but I wished I could have shared the occasion with her and known for myself of her approval. Three weeks after our ceremony in the Salt Lake Temple, I had a dream in the middle of the night, and in that dream I left the earth.

At first I was in a palatial salon that was symbolic of the earth. It was filled with heavy baroque furniture and crowded with people who were laughing and talking. I was moving around in this party with my husband, yet constantly aware of a tremendous downward gravitational pull on me toward the ground. The furnishings, as well as the ideas discussed, were heavy and earthy.

As we mingled among the guests at this party, I suddenly felt that I *had* to leave and was pulled by some unseen force toward a giant stairway that went up in two directions against one wall. I went up the right-hand side, next to a huge, darkly painted mural of the luscious things of the earth — fruits, flowers, and beautiful people. I was holding my husband's hand, but the force pulling at me was so great that I was simply propelled up the stairway. I kept holding his hand over the railing as long as possible, and then I knew that I had to go on up that stairway, leaving all that I saw below me.

I went up the stairs as they became darker and darker until I could not see where I was putting my feet as I lifted them for the next step. Finally, I was completely separated from the earth, lost in total, darkened oblivion.

Then a small light appeared far ahead, illuminating my steps as I neared it. I moved from the darkness into a building with three full arches on the left-hand side, just barely discernible in their brightness. On each side behind me was a personage, propelling me forward and insisting with their unspoken force that I go into the next hall.

When I started toward the doorway through the open arches into what I was given to understand was a temple annex, I realized that I was walking absolutely effortlessly above the ground. It was such a great contrast to the heaviness I had experienced on the earth. I could move at will. Even though the people were propelling me from behind, I felt totally comfortable with them as I skimmed across the surface of that beautiful white floor.

As I went forward, I passed through an anteroom toward a huge, long room reaching far, far to my left beneath a barrel vault. I was in the end of that room, toward the right, where a glorious fan-shaped window filled the end above the first twenty feet of solid wall. The window and entire ceiling were made of pearlescent glass — the most iridescent, pale, rainbow-colored and subtle-toned glass that I have ever seen. Each piece was in the shape of leaves or flowers and held together in a manner similar to our stained-glass windows here, but with the glass lacework spreading in naturalistic, curving, organic designs.

The light spreading down through that ceiling was the most overwhelming experience I can recall in my whole life. It filtered in to fill the whole room, everything and everybody.

To my left down the center length of this room were thirty-foot ferns stretching farther than I could see in an unbroken line. I was astonished at their lovely size. To my right, beneath the fan-shaped window, were creamy-white desks of simple design. People sat at a few of the desks keeping some sort of records.

Then people began coming out of the archways ahead of me on the other side of the room. I was given to understand, without any words being spoken, that they were coming out of a temple. As they came out, they stopped at a desk and informed the people at the desk about what they had been doing in the temple, and the people recorded it. Thirty-six years ago, when I had this experience in the spring of 1951, I remember trying to describe the typewriters the workers were using. They were little low keyboards that I now realize were computer keyboards, or something very similar to that, but without the bulky boxes that hold our computer screens.

As I marvelled over this, out of the group from the temple came my mother! I was filled with joy at the thought that my desire could now be satiated, for I could ask her if she approved of the man I had chosen. She saw me and stopped still, without moving toward me for a few seconds. Her face showed that she was horrified to see me, because, I'm sure, she thought I'd died and arrived in the spirit world for good.

Mother looked just as I remember her, with her same sympathetic face, brown eyes, gray hair. I was her last child, and her hair had been graying even from my earliest memories.

She wore a robe of a beautiful, dark, sky blue. A drape of her favorite rose color was bordered in gold and hung over one shoulder. It struck me as looking quite medieval, but comfortable and graceful. All the people coming out of the temple were wearing very beautiful robes and dresses of rich, polychrome colors.[1]

My mother finally recovered herself and came forward. She gazed intently into my eyes , not embracing me, but eagerly clasping my hands. I did not converse with her in words. We communicated easily, in an instantaneous and deep-from-the-heart way that was very wonderful and comforting. She was happy with what I had done in my life. I was able to ask her how she felt about my marriage, and then I was propelled away.

I held onto my mother's hands as long as possible, until the force of my escorts required that I leave. I was being propelled a little more upward all the time, into a blinding light, and then I found myself in my own bed, as if I were awakening from a dream. I immediately woke my husband and shared my joy with him. For

---

[1]It is interesting to note that Carma is a costumer by profession.

days I was in such an ecstasy that I could not concentrate on the things of this world.

Carma's visit with her mother and the beauty of the spirit world was understandably exhilarating. We know from many other sources as well that the beauty and wonder of that world defy description. Consider the many similarities between Carma's account and the following one, as told by Heber C. Kimball:

> I went to see him [Jedediah M. Grant] one day last week. ...he could not speak, but he shook hands warmly with me...
> I laid my hands upon him and blessed him, and asked God to strengthen his lungs that he might [breathe] easier, and in two or three minutes he raised himself up and talked for about an hour as busily as he could, telling me what he had seen and what he understood, until I was afraid he would weary himself when I arose and left him.
> He said to me, Brother Heber, I have been into the spirit world two nights in succession and, of all the dreads that ever came across me, the worst was to have to again return to my body, though I had to do it. But O, says he, the order of righteous men and women; I beheld them organized in their several grades, and there appeared to be no obstruction to my vision...I looked to see whether there was any disorder there, but there was none; neither could I see any death nor any darkness, disorder or confusion. He said that the people he there saw were organized in family capacities; and when he looked at them he saw grade after grade, and all were organized and in

harmony. He would mention one item after another and say, "Why, it is just as Brother Brigham says it is; it is just as he has told us many a time..."

He saw the righteous gathered together in the spirit world and there were not wicked spirits among them. He saw his wife; she was the first person that came to him. He saw many that he knew, but did not have conversation with any except his wife Caroline. She came to him, and he said that she looked beautiful and had their little child, that died on the Plains, in her arms and said, "Mr. Grant, here is little Margaret; you know that the wolves ate her up, but it did not hurt her; here she is all right."

"To my astonishment," he said, "when I looked at families there was a deficiency in some, there was a lack, for I saw families that would not be permitted to come and dwell together, because they had not honored their calling here..."

He also spoke of the buildings he saw there, remarking that the Lord gave Solomon wisdom and poured gold and silver into his hands that he might display his skill and ability, and said that the temple erected by Solomon was much inferior to the most ordinary buildings he saw in the spirit world.

In regard to gardens, says Brother Grant, "I have seen good gardens on this earth, but I never saw any to compare with those that were there. I saw flowers of numerous kinds, and some with from fifty to a hundred different colored flowers growing upon one stalk." We have many kinds of flowers on the earth, and I suppose those very articles came from heaven, or they would not be here.

After mentioning the things that he had seen, he spoke of how much he disliked to return and resume his body, after having seen the beauty and glory of the spirit world, where the righteous spirits are gathered together.

Some may marvel at my speaking about these things, for many profess to believe that we have no spiritual existence. But do you not believe that my spirit was organized before it came to my body here? And do you not think there can be houses and gardens, fruit trees, and every other thing there? The spirits of those things were made, as well as our spirits, and it follows that they can exist upon the same principle.[2]

After speaking of the gardens and the beauty of everything there, Brother Grant said that he felt extremely sorrowful at having to leave so beautiful a place and come back to earth, for he looked upon his body with loathing, but was obliged to enter it again.

He said that after he came back he could look upon his family and see the spirit that was in them, and the darkness that was in them; and that he conversed with them about the gospel, and what they should do, and they replied, "Well, Brother Grant, perhaps it is so, and perhaps it is not," and said that was the state of this

---

[2]This is the principle of duality, that all things were created spiritually before they were created physically upon the earth. Speaking of God's creations, Genesis 2:5 says, "And every plant of the field before it was in the earth, and every herb of the field before it grew: for the Lord God had not caused it to rain upon the earth and there was not a man to till the ground." How could man not be there to till if we already know of his creation, and how could plants and herbs exist before their creation if not in spirit? See also McConkie, Bruce R., (Comp.)*Doctrines of Salvation--Sermons and Writings of Joseph Fielding Smith*, Vol. 1, pp. 63-64.

people to a great extent, for many are full of darkness and will not believe me.[3]

It is interesting to think about the underlying importance of family in these descriptions of the spirit world environment. Jose's grandmother, Carma's mother, and Brother Grant's wife — all relatives — came to greet them. While Jose saw houses like cottages, and Carma and Brother Grant saw magnificent edifices, each building indicated organization by family, especially the prevalence of temples, because that is the place for establishing eternal family ties.[4] A beautiful family home in the spirit world is described in this account of Nola's:

> During a very troubled part of my life when my health was poor, my marriage floundering, and I was struggling with a wild teenager, I became quite depressed. Then the news reached me that my father was ill, perhaps dying. At that point when I had sunk to my lowest ebb of anxiety, I had this dream.
>
> I was entering a lovely room with high ceilings and arches. The decor was in shades of beige and cream, and other soft colors, but mostly light, warm colors of white. The home was spacious, but it was also connected to many long hallways, doorways, walls and corners. The architecture

---

[3]Burton, *For They Shall Be Comforted*, pp. 82-84.

[4]Especially consider Brother Grant's comments: ". . .the people he saw there were organized in family capacities; and when he looked at them he saw grade after grade, and all were organized in perfect harmony." And later, " . . . there was a deficiency in some [families], there was a lack, for I saw families that would not be permitted to come and dwell together, because they had not honored their calling here."

was beautiful, different from anything I had ever seen or have seen since. There were long, curving corridors with couch-seats built into the walls that you could sit on and look out the lovely windows into gardens and far-away landscapes.

On some walls were practical things that had been designed as art work. For instance, I saw large letters that hung in colorful combinations on the walls and were used for teaching.

I was going to see my father, and suddenly I found him there. He was very happy to see me and gave me a big smile and said,

"Come over here, I want to show you my big house." It was his custom in life to show me his house whenever I would come to visit. He would show me what he had improved in the garden or how he had redecorated or whatever. It was a familiar feeling for me as I followed him on a tour.

I also saw a machine, run by a keyboard, that gathered material at people's request. Rather than leafing through volumes of books, as they requested things, the machine would drop down and return with the information. I had never seen nor heard of a computer at the time, but this machine was similar to one.

A wonderful organ projected colors and patterns along with the music played on it. My father played it with great skill and joy, and the organ and the colors it projected related to the decor of this wonderful building.

We had a wonderful time as my father showed me around, though there were many rooms I didn't look into because there were people busy in them. We stayed in the main portion of the building, and, at one point, my father pulled back a curtain of some sort so we could peek down at a gorgeous swimming pool of all different shades of blue. I don't know what this free-form pool was used for, but it was very lovely just to look at.

I was thrilled to see this wonderful place. I knew that my children, my grandchildren, all my grandchildren's children, and everybody could come to this family institution, which seemed to be Daddy's place, only it was related to many groups of people in the same way as the halls and rooms branched off throughout it.

Then I thought, "Wow, this is a lot of stuff to manage, to clean, to maintain," and I started thinking about it all in a worldly sense. I asked my father, "How do you take care of all of this?"

He smiled and his eyes were bright as he said, with the most airy attitude, "Oh, we *can* and we *do*."

And I didn't worry about it any more.

Then I had a lovely experience arranging some blue glass objects. They were movable, flexible pieces of blue glass. I am always arranging people's flowers and things here, and I guess it was the same there,[5] since I got to arrange these clear, lily-like forms of glass. Without punching buttons or turning switches or seeing cords, lights would come on in the glass to compliment the arrangement I had made, like a lamp that didn't need electricity.

After I had finished, we went on, and there were many windows in the curved corridors that became rooms, and through others we could see

---

[5]It is fascinating to note how Nola's current artistic talents shaped her perceptions in the next world, so that the things she noticed most had to do with visual aspects and her own artistic inclinations.

landscapes, beautiful simple scenes in lovely color combinations. Some were of the mortal world and some looked onto higher planes.

My dream ended, but I awoke with my personal anxieties gone. I felt content that when my father did pass away, this would be his place in paradise. It would be a lovely family home where we would all go until we settle into wherever we will be through the eternities. Here we would be able to contact our loved ones and extended family. We would talk with them, get reassurance, and be satisfied. It is to be a place of luxury and grandeur for the extended family; yet cozy to individuals.

This dream was a great comfort to me, a hope for the next life, and a motivation to live this mortal life the best I can.

Nola's dream was of a splendid family house in the next life. In the following brief description, Annie saw the mansion that would be hers:

I can't tell you whether this experience is an out-of-the-body one, a dream, or a vision, but it is like Nephi wondering whether he was really dreaming or whether he was beyond the veil, seeing things of the future.

Grandmother had an experience where she was in the next life. My grandfather had not even died yet, but she saw the mansion that she and grandfather were to have. She was not necessarily led by anybody; she was just there. Everything surrounding this mansion was absolutely perfect, the landscaping satisfying and pleasing to the eye.

Grandmother was immediately impressed to go inside, and so she walked into this very, very large mansion. There were many rooms with marble walls and floors like crystal glass. She gazed about her at the exquisite beauty for some time, entirely overcome by the loveliness of her reward. The thing that impressed her the most was that as she looked through the walls within one large room, she noticed a rose set into the marble. As the marble was quite clear in this spot, she saw roses that were actually alive, with dew on them, inside the marble. Grandmother wept at the beauty.

These descriptions of vast and awe-inspiring buildings are given credence by the Savior's statement, "In my Father's house are many mansions...I go to prepare a place for you. And...I will come again, and receive you unto myself; that where I am there ye may be also."[6] Without doubt, the spirit world is a breathtaking panorama of beauty displaying our Heavenly Father's love.

---

[6]John 14:2-3. See also Enos 1:27 and D&C 76:111.

Questions and Answers

1. What does the spirit world look like? Do descriptions differ?

According to scripture, the temporal world is fashioned after the spirit world:

> Thus the heaven and the earth were finished, and all the host of them.
>
> And every plant of the field before it was in the earth, and every herb of the field before it grew. For I, the Lord God, created all things, of which I have spoken, spiritually, before they were naturally upon the face of the earth. (Moses 3:1,5)

Jedediah M. Grant's account of the spirit world told in this chapter illustrates this principle of duality.[7] He said that he had seen beautiful gardens here on the earth, but that he had never seen any to compare with those of the spirit world. Then he asked if it was any wonder that it was so familiar, since the spirit of everything on the earth was first created there, although he implied that it was natural for there to be some things he had never seen in

---

[7]In relationship to the idea of duality, it is helpful to understand that a concept of the spirit world as one large area is not correct. President Brigham Young indicated this and its relationship with the principle of progression when he said, "And when we passed into that sphere where Joseph is, there is still another department, and then another, and another, and so on to an eternal progression in exaltation and eternal lives. That is the exaltation I am looking for." Brigham Young, *Journal of Discourses*, Vol. 3, p. 375.

mortality, such as the flowers of numerous colors growing upon one stalk.

We may conclude, that the next world is much more like this mortal one than traditional notions suggest. Indeed, Dr. Moody, reported that out of all his subjects, no one described winged, harp-playing angels, or a hell of flames with demons and pitchforks. Still, the descriptions of the spirit world given in this chapter, like Brother Grant's, are varied and colorful. Accounts differ because perceptions vary, and sometimes what is seen is so indescribable that it cannot be clearly explained. In spite of this wide variation in accounts, the recurring theme is that no one seems anxious to leave. Ella Jensen expressed the feelings of most visitors when she said that as soon as she had a glimpse of the spirit world she was anxious to remain and all care and worry left her:

> I entered a large hall. It was so long that I could not see the end of it. It was filled with people...I passed on through the room and met many of my relatives and friends. It was like going along the crowded streets of a city where you meet many people, only a very few of whom you recognize...Everybody appeared perfectly happy.[8]

Upon death, then, we can look forward to visiting a place whose environment is similar to our physical world. It was organized before this world, just as were the spirits of men, beasts, plants, and all

---

[8]Leroi C. Snow, "Raised from the Dead," *Improvement Era*, Vol. 32, no. 12, October, 1929, pp. 973-974.

living things. It appears that there are houses, gardens, fruit trees, and many other things of which all earthly things are only a similitude.

2. *What are the purposes of buildings in the spirit world?*

Buildings of some type are described by many who have gone beyond the veil. In some cases, they have clearly defined purpose such as housing computer-like terminals, serving as meeting places for children or adults, or separating and providing sanctuary for myriads of spirit beings. In other cases, spirits are allowed to see and experience being in the company of other spirits and mortals in the buildings belonging to our own physical world.

In this chapter, Carma and Nola gave vivid descriptions of buildings with elaborate furnishings and draperies. Annie's simple account of a living rose within a marble wall inspires as much awe in us as Brother Grant's indication that Solomon's Temple would pale in comparison to the buildings he saw. These descriptions mesh well with the following account given by David P. Kimball:

> (I was taken into) a vast building, which was built on the plan of the Order of Zion. I entered through a south door and found myself in a part of the building which was unfinished, though a great many workmen were busy upon it. My guide showed me all through this half of the house, and then took me through the other half which was finished. The richness, grandeur and beauty of it defied description. There were many apartments in the house, which was very spa-

cious, and they differed in size and the fineness of workmanship according to the merits on earth of those who were to occupy them. I felt most at home in the unfinished part, among the workmen. The upper part of the house was filled with saints, but I could not see them, though some of them conversed with me. . . .[9]

In his account, George Ritchie described an enormous building in a gorgeous, sunny park where there was a relationship between all the structures — a pattern to the way things were arranged. He described entering one of the buildings and moving down a high-ceilinged corridor lined with tall doorways. The atmosphere of the place was that of a tremendous study center or library with wide halls and curving stairways. He glimpsed enormous rooms filled with detailed equipment, intricate charts, complicated controls and consoles. And, like Carma and Nola, he saw all of this long before the advent of the computer age! He described visiting other buildings, like a studio where very complex music was being composed and performed, a space observatory, and a vast library filled with documents on parchment, clay, leather, metal, and other materials. At the very apex of George Ritchie's experience, he reported seeing a "city of light."[10]

Although it is difficult to draw definite conclusions regarding the buildings of the spirit world, it is clear that many who have visited there have

---

[9]Whitney, "A Terrible Ordeal," *Helpful Visions*, p. 13.

[10]Ritchie, *Return From Tomorrow*, p. 69.

vivid recollections of them, and after considering enough of their stories, we find that we have a general feel for their uses and impressive workmanship.

3. *How much are spirits with friends and relatives?*

In light of our understanding of Paradise and Spirit Prison we can answer this question by considering whether or not a certain spirit is assigned to Paradise or Spirit Prison, and whether or not his friends and relatives are in the same place.

We can also reflect on the overwhelming number of experiences with the spirit world that refer to being with friends and relatives. Brigham Young said:

> We have more friends behind the veil than on this side, and they will hail us more joyfully than you were ever welcomed by your parents and friends in this world; and you will rejoice more when you meet them than you ever rejoiced to see a friend in this life.[11]

Joseph F. Smith explained:

> (When someone dies he has) returned nearer to the home circles, to old associations and scenes, much in the same way as a man who comes home from a foreign mission to join again

---

[11]Brigham Young, *Journal of Discourses*, Vol. 6, p. 349.

his family and friends and enjoy the pleasures and comforts of home.[12]

Based on these commentaries, we can be certain that our assumptions about relationships with family and friends in the next life are accurate. However, we must consider that all the experiences in this book have come from people who have been reasonably committed to religious values and teachings. It may be that those who do not share these values could have a more negative experience in the next world. For example, there is no evidence that there are strong family ties there for those who do not value them at all in this life.[13] We know of no one like this who has had a spirit world experience, and the same seems to be true for others who have studied the next life.

4. Is time measured in the spirit world?

Joseph Smith was once asked, "Is not the reckoning of God's time, angel's time, prophet's time, and man's time, according to the planet on which they reside?" and he answered, "Yes." He also said that immortal beings reside where all things for their glory are manifest whether past, present, or future, and are continually before the Lord (see D&C 130:4-7).

---

[12]Smith, *Gospel Doctrine*, p. 440.

[13]In fact, Jedediah M. Grant asserted that there are families who "would not be permitted to come and dwell together, because they had not honored their calling here."

Many accounts of the spirit world indicate that time is not sensed there[14] and Elder Neal A. Maxwell, of the Council of the Twelve Apostles, has explained such feelings in this way:

> When the veil which now encloses us is no more, time will also be no more (See D&C 84:100). Even now, time is clearly not our natural dimension. Thus we are never really at home in time. Alternately, we find ourselves impatiently wishing to hasten the passage of time or to hold back the dawn. We can do neither, of course. Whereas the bird is at home in the air, we are clearly not at home in time — because we belong to eternity! Time, as much as any one thing, whispers to us that we are strangers here. If time were natural to us, why is it that we have so many clocks and wear wristwatches?[15]

5. *What type of government or authority exists in the spirit world?*

Government:

Since earthly things are patterned after heavenly things, and because the Lord admonishes us to establish a house of order repeatedly in the Doctrine and Covenants, it stands to reason that some type of government or organization must exist in the spirit world. In fact, since the restoration, the Lord's prophets have clearly taught that the government

---

[14]This was underscored by Dr. Moody's research in *Life After Life*, p. 47.

[15]Neal A. Maxwell, "Patience," *Ensign*, October 1980, p. 31.

of the spirit world is similar to the church government on earth — a theocracy. Joseph Smith said:

> The spirits of men are eternal, that they are *governed* by the same priesthood that Abraham, Melchizedek, and the Apostles were: that they are *organized* according to that priesthood which is everlasting...that they all move in their respective spheres, and are *governed* by the law of God; that when they appear upon the earth they are in a probationary state, and are preparing, if righteous, for a future and greater glory....[16]

Power and Authority:

In his vision of the spirit world, President Joseph F. Smith saw that the Savior organized his forces from among the righteous, giving them *authority and power* to go forth and teach the gospel to the spirits of all men. He further saw that when faithful elders depart mortality, they continue that work by joining those faithful ones who preceded them (see D&C 138:33, 59).

President John Taylor taught that there is a connecting link between the priesthood on earth and in heaven. Those men who held the priesthood and used it faithfully on earth are also using it in heaven.[17] Brigham Young stated:

> When we pass into the spirit world we shall possess a measure of this power; not to that de-

---

[16]Joseph Smith, *History of the Church*, Vol. 4, pp. 575-576. Note Jedediah M. Grant's remarks on organization, in this chapter.

[17]John Taylor as quoted by Burton, *For They Shall Be Comforted*, p. 80.

gree that we will when resurrected and brought forth in the fullness of glory to inherit the kingdoms prepared for us. The power the faithful will possess then will far exceed that of the spirit world; but that enjoyed in the spirit world is so far beyond this life as to be inconceivable without the spirit of revelation.[18]

Leadership:

It appears that the ultimate authority or governing power in the next world rests with the Savior. In turn, he holds the head prophet of each dispensation responsible for administering the affairs relating to the people of his time period. They report through Adam to Christ. Wilford Woodruff taught that Joseph Smith holds the keys of this dispensation, "and every apostle, every seventy, every elder, etc., who has died in the faith as soon as he passes to the other side of the veil, enters into the work of the ministry..."[19]

Governing bodies similar to the First Presidency and the Quorum of the Twelve Apostles seem to exist there, as we will see in personal accounts to come.

Delegation and Stewardship:

It appears that a spirit must either be given an assignment or be granted permission to visit mortals. Since the same procedure is followed in the

---

[18]Brigham Young, *Journal of Discourses*, Vol. 14, p. 231.

[19]Wilford Woodruff as quoted by Burton, *For They Shall Be Comforted*, p. 80.

earthly church, it should not be surprising that spirits mention having permission to come.

It also seems that permission and authority must be given to spirits to call someone from this mortal sphere to the spirit world. As we read more accounts, there will be situations where a spirit grants someone permission to return to mortality, but let us note a few examples where people have not returned.

President Wilford Woodruff tells of a time when Bishop Roskelley was taken seriously ill and visited by President Peter Maughan from the spirit world. President Maughan told him that they had held a council on the other side of the veil, and that he had come to appoint a man to return with and help them. When he told Bishop Roskelley that he was one of them, the Bishop began to tell him about all he had to do. President Maughan said, "I think I will not call you. I think you are wanted here more than perhaps one of the others." Soon a second man was taken sick, but he recovered and repeated a similar story to Bishop Roskelley's. A few days later, a third man was taken sick and died. President Woodruff said, "Now I name this to show a principle. They have work on the other side of the veil; and they want men, and they call them."[20]

In a similar instance, Edward J. Wood tells of an out-of-body experience he had in which he met his uncle Henry, who told of his busy life in the spirit world. He had been engaged in missionary work

---

[20]Wilford Woodruff, *Journal of Discourses*, Vol. 22, pp. 333-334.

and told President Wood the names of six men who had just been called to help there. Since three of the six men were still serving on the Alberta Stake high council, President Wood was deeply puzzled. Within a period of a few weeks, each of the three men had died.[21]

In conclusion, there is organization and authority in the spirit world similar to what we have in the mortal church. Those who live there are not totally free to do as they wish, but are subject to that authority in their actions.

---

[21]Melvin S. Tagg, *The Life of Edward James Wood.* Provo, Ut.: Masters Thesis, Brigham Young University, 1959, pp. 90-92.

6

The Return

One striking similarity between the accounts of people returning from the dead is their obvious reluctance. At times they feel an initial and very great concern about children or loved ones in mortality, but it seems even then, that their desire to return weakens in proportion to how long they have been in the spirit world. Richard shared with us the following experience:

> My mother's aunt was an elderly lady whose husband had already passed on. One day she suddenly got sick and died. No one was prepared for her death, but in about three or four hours, all her children had gathered together. One of her sons was a stake president and two or three of them were bishops in Brigham City, Corinne, and the Bear River area of Utah. The sons decided they did not want their mother to be dead, so they

laid their hands upon her head and gave her a blessing and called her back.

My mother's aunt came back, but it was a very bad thing for the family. Prior to her death, even though she was elderly, she was able to get around by herself. After they called her back, she was bedridden for the rest of her life.

She had been gone between two and four hours and had conversed with her husband, her mother and father, and brothers and sisters that had already passed on. While she was visiting with her family, somebody informed her that she would have to go back. She said she did not want to, but she had no choice. Her descriptions of them, dressed in white, were vivid. She had recognized them all.

Mother's aunt was extremely angry with her kids. She told them over and over that her death had been the most peaceful experience in the world. I guess everyone was pretty upset. Her children asked for a report on how this relative and that relative was doing — and they got it! Their mother kept telling them that when people die, let them go. She knew that her sons had great faith and were just not ready to let her go, but she never forgave them for bringing her back.

In the following brief journal entry, Jacob Hamblin explains how the mortal world appeared to him and describes his reluctance to return to earth once he was in the spirit world:

During the summer of 1858, when I was at my home on the Santa Clara, one morning about nine o'clock, while engaged in cutting some of the large branches from a cottonwood tree, I fell a distance of twenty or thirty feet to the ground. I was badly bruised, and was carried to my house for dead, or nearly so.

I came to my senses about eight o'clock in the evening, and threw off from my stomach quite a quantity of blood. I requested the brethren who were standing around to administer to me, and they did so. From the time I fell from the tree until then was lost to me, so far as earthly matters were concerned.

During the time my body lay in this condition, it seemed to me that I went up from the earth and looked down upon it, and it appeared like a dark ball.[1]

The overwhelming desire that visitors have to remain in the world even carries over into situations where the individual has not led as good a life as he ought, and it would appear that he would be more wise to return and right his wrongs. When he visited the spirit world, Alphaeus Cutler did not want to return, though he had to. He eventually formed the apostate "True Church of Latter-day Saints," but when he was an old man, he bore this testimony to his grandson, Abraham A. Kimball:

I know that Joseph Smith was a prophet of God, and I know that Brigham Young is his legal successor, and I always did know it. But the trouble with me was I wanted to lead, and could not

---

[1] Crowther, *Life Everlasting*, pp. 75-76. He went on to add that, "the place where I was seemed very desirable to remain in. It was divided into compartments by walls, from which appeared to grow out vines and flowers, displaying an endless variety of colors."

be led. I have run my race and sealed my doom, and I know what I have got to meet.

I died once, and was dead for some length of time. My spirit left my body and went to the land of spirits. I saw the crown that I should wear if I remained faithful, and the condemnation I should receive if I did not. I begged to remain, but was informed that I must return and warn the people to repent, as my work on earth was not yet done.[2]

We cannot help but wonder if Alphaeus knew his own weaknesses well enough to anticipate his future actions and to shrink from the testing that was yet to be his in mortality.

Whatever their reasons, it is obvious in returned-from-the-dead experiences, that no one blithely chooses to be restored to their body. Rather, such decisions usually exhibit selfless concern for loved ones and/or devotion to the work of the Lord.

My mother Margaret, was a young lady when her appendix ruptured. Later, peritonitis set in and she died.

---

[2]Alphaeus went on to tell his grandson that, "After my spirit returned to my body, those around discovered the appearance of life. The first words that I spoke were to Sidney Rigdon, who was stooping over me. I called upon him to repent of his sins, or he woud be damned." Alphaeus continued by admonishing his grandson to remain "steadfast to Mormonism," and "Let what may turn up, never yield the point; for it will save and exalt you in the kingdom of God." His grandson remarks, "He wept like a child after saying this. . .then said to me, 'One favor I wish to ask of you, namely, that you will not divulge this confession to those whom I lead while I live.'" Abraham A. Kimball, "Finding a Father," *Gems for the Young Folks*, Salt Lake City, Ut.: Juvenile Instructor's Office, 1881, pp. 16-17.

When she left her body, she was met by a heavenly being who told her that she had a decision to make. Because her mother had previously passed away, leaving a large family, her father needed her very much. She was also aware that her older sister and brothers were bearing great responsibilities and needed her help.

The person who met her said, "You can go back into your body, or remain here. It is your choice."

My mother looked around her and saw that everything was beautiful and peaceful. She was overwhelmed with the joy and relief that would have been hers if she had stayed there. Mother also saw her father weeping and trying to comfort her grieving brothers and sisters.

After serious consideration, she felt her family needed her in mortality. She often mentioned to me how hard it was to decide to return to the pain and suffering of the earth, but that is what she did.

She tried many times to describe the beauties of that place and the peaceful feeling she had there, but it was always beyond words. She experienced terrible pain and suffering in returning to her body. Coming back was similar to the way it feels when your arm goes to sleep and then starts tingling as the blood begins to circulate again. But this sensation was intensified, it was only part of her pain, and it covered her entire body.

In 1838, Phoebe Woodruff was given a choice of remaining in the spirit world or returning to mortality. Her choice is another excellent example of the selflessness and devotion that usually accom-

panies the decision to come back. Wilford
Woodruff describes the situation:

> December 3 found my wife very low. I spent
> the day in taking care of her, and the day follow-
> ing I returned to Eaton to get some things for her.
> She seemed to be sinking gradually, and in the
> evening the spirit apparently left her body, and
> she was dead. The sisters gathered around, weep-
> ing, while I stood looking at her in sorrow. The
> spirit and power of God began to rest upon me
> until, for the first time during her sickness, faith
> filled my soul, although she lay before me as one
> dead.
>
> I had some oil that was consecrated for my
> anointing while in Kirtland. I took it and con-
> secrated it again before the Lord, for anointing the
> sick. I then bowed down before the Lord, prayed
> for the life of my companion, and in the name of
> the Lord anointed her body with the oil. I then
> laid my hands upon her, and in the name of
> Jesus Christ I rebuked the power of death and of
> the destroyer, and commanded the same to de-
> part from her and the spirit of life to enter her
> body. Her spirit returned to her body, and from
> that hour she was made whole; and we all felt to
> praise the name of God, and to trust in Him and
> keep His commandments.
>
> While I was undergoing this ordeal (as my
> wife related afterward) her spirit left her body,
> and she saw it lying upon the bed and the sisters
> there weeping. She looked at them and at me,
> and upon her babe. While gazing upon this
> scene, two persons came into the room, carrying
> a coffin, and told her they had come for her body.
> One of these messengers said to her that she

might have her choice — she might go to rest in the spirit world, or, upon one condition, she could have the privilege of returning to her tabernacle and of continuing her labors upon the earth. The condition was that if she felt she could stand by her husband, and with him pass through all the cares, trials, tribulations, and afflictions of life which he would be called upon to pass through for the gospel's sake unto the end, she might return. When she looked at the situation of her husband and child she said, "Yes, I will do it." At the moment the decision was made the power of faith rested upon me, and when I administered to her, her spirit re-entered her tabernacle, and she saw the messengers carry the coffin out the door.[3]

These experiences suggest that death and the journey beyond are something good men and women have no need to fear. Eddie Rickenbacker put it this way:

You may have heard that dying is unpleasant, but don't believe it. Dying is the sweetest, tenderest, most sensuous sensation I have ever experienced. Death comes disguised as a sympathetic friend. All was serene; all was calm. How wonderful it would be simply to float out of this world. It is easy to die. You have to fight to live.[4]

---

[3]Wilford Woodruff, "Leaves From my Journal," (Third Book in the Faith Promoting Series, Fourth edition), *The Deseret News*, 1909, pp. 59-60.

[4]Edward Rickenbacker, *The Autobiography of Eddie Rickenbacker.* Englewood Cliffs, N.J.: Prentice-Hall, 1967, p. 243.

Questions and Answers

1. What do we know about the spirit-body relationship?

The Role of the Spirit:

The spirit activates and controls the body, not the reverse. Heber C. Kimball taught that the spirit remains the same after leaving the body as it was before. But the physical senses of the body and various body organs no longer operate. The very second the spirit leaves, life is gone, and the body begins to decompose.[5]

We have already read several out-of-the-body experiences, and any of these substantiate the life-giving relationship of the spirit to the body. Consider the role of the spirit in the following account by John Peterson. You may recall our earlier reference to his story, in which he described dying, noting that his father sat beside his body, apparently unmoved and unaware:

> With a bow we started to return and, seemingly, but a short space of time had elapsed ere we reached home, and standing by the bed, where my body lay, my guide touched my hands, the spirit entered the body at that instant, the blood commenced to circulate warmly through my veins, and in a few minutes I felt my lungs ex-

---

[5]Heber C. Kimball as quoted by Burton, *For They Shall Be Comforted*, p. 70.

panding. As I stood upon the floor I noticed the clock; the hands pointed to four o'clock in the morning, so I had been absent between five and six hours. My father was still reading. I spoke to him. Said he, "My boy, I thought you were dead." I said, "I was, Father."[6]

A Time to Die:

And again, it shall come to pass that he that hath faith in me to be healed, and is not appointed unto death, shall be healed. (D&C 42:48)

To every thing there is a season, and a time to every purpose under the heaven:
A time to be born, and a time to die....(Ecclesiastes 3:1-2)

These two scriptures indicate that there is a set time when each man must die. It is clear from the first scripture that if a person is not "appointed unto death" and there is sufficient faith, his life can be spared, but Spencer W. Kimball taught that many die before their time because there is not enough faith. He explained that we can also shorten our lifes by making foolish decisions, but only rarely can we lengthen them.[7] Joseph Fielding Smith also cautioned that while some people are "called home," we should not conclude that all

---

[6]Peterson, "Was Dead and Came to Life Again," *Millenial Star*, Vol. 68, 1916, p. 699.

[7]Spencer W. Kimball, *Tragedy or Destiny?* Salt Lake City, Ut.: Deseret Book, Co., 1977, p. 9.

deaths are divinely appointed.[8] In fact, Heber J. Grant specifically mentions that there are many Latter-day Saints who in sickness give up and die before their appointed time and before finishing their labors here.[9]

From these teachings we can see that if sufficient faith were exercised, many of us could remain and finish the work of our mortal probation. So it should not be surprising, to consider that some of those who have near-death experiences are allowed to return because they were *directed* to, or were *given permission* to, or were *called back by priesthood authority* on this side.

Death is a Temporary Separation of the Body from the Spirit:

Without the body, the spirit is not perfect. We are taught in the Doctrine and Covenants:

> For man is spirit. The elements are eternal, and spirit and element, inseparably connected, receive a fulness of joy; And when separated, man cannot receive a fullness of joy. (D&C 93:33-34)

> For as ye have looked upon the long absence of your spirits from your bodies to be a bondage, I will show unto you how the day of redemption shall come. . . . (D&C 45:17)

---

[8]Smith, *Answers to Gospel Questions*, Vol. 3, p. 48.

[9]Heber J. Grant, in Conference Report, Oct. 1899, p. 35.

These verses explain that the separation of the body from the spirit is a period of incompleteness. However, there would be no purpose in having a body, if it were not to be restored in the Resurrection. And there would be no advantage in having a Resurrection if the body came forth with the same imperfections it had when it was laid down. In the Resurrection our bodies will be perfected, free from disease and deformity.

2. *Why are so many reluctant to return to their bodies?*

In the first story in this chapter, the woman who was called back was not only reluctant to return, but even resentful. It seems that this was her appointed time to die, and having been called back, she was left bedridden for the rest of her life. Her feelings were not unusual, since no one in this chapter seems to have wanted to return, probably because of the overwhelming feelings of peace and serenity they were enjoying. Those who choose to come back only do it for some explicit purpose.

3. *For what reasons do they return?*

From examples in this chapter and others we have gathered, we see three reasons why people return:

They are called back by priesthood authority:

The scriptures give us many examples of these, and among them are the times the Savior restored the spirit to the body of the daughter of Jairus (see

Mark 5:35-42), to the son of the widow of Nain (see
Luke 7:12-16), and to Lazarus (see John 11:1-44), all
through His priesthood authority.

When President Lorenzo Snow called Ella
Jensen's spirit back to her body two hours after she
died, he told her parents to wait and not to mourn
because everything would be all right. He left, and
more than an hour had passed when Ella opened
her eyes and looked around the room.

> "Where is he?" she said. "Who?" those about
> her asked, "Where is who?" "Why, Brother
> Snow," she said, "He called me back...Why did he
> call me back? I was so happy and did not want to
> come. . . ."[10]

*They are directed to return by someone in the
spirit world:*

Alphaeus Cutler begged to remain in the spirit
world, but was given no choice. Another instance
of being directed to return is found in the firm request of Walter P. Monson's daughter when her
spirit met his on the other side of the veil:

> "Go back, Papa, I want Richard first. Then
> Grandma must come, and then Mama is coming,
> before you."[11]

*They request and are given permission to re-
turn:*

---

[10]Snow, "Raised from the Dead," pp. 885-886.

[11]Hackworth, *The Master's Touch*, p. 61.

In his extensive study, Dr. Moody found that many individuals felt they were allowed to return because there was still some mission for them to perform.[12] In Chapter 4, one woman was restored to life because she had agreed to be part of a great missionary effort and in coming chapters we will read about individuals who returned in order to do their family's genealogy work. Perhaps the most common reason people choose to return, however, is because of the responsibility they feel toward their immediate mortal family.

David P. Kimball was lost and dying of thirst in the Arizona desert when his deceased father came to him. After being reproved for his earthly conduct, David was told he could come ahead to the spirit world if he wanted to:

> I pled with him that I might stay with my family long enough to make them comfortable, to repent of my sins, and more fully prepare myself for the change. Had it not been for this, I never should have returned home, except as a corpse. He finally told me I could remain two years, and to do all the good I could during that time, after which he would come for me.[13]

In summary then, there are three reasons why disembodied spirits return to mortality. Clearly, whatever the reason is, it must be according to the authority and with the permission of those holding the keys.

---

[12]Moody, *Life After Life*, p. 79-80.

[13]Whitney, *Helpful Visions*, p. 14.

SECTION IV

Spirit World Activities

7

Missionary Work

Ask any Latter-day Saint what spirits do, and you will be likely to get an answer similar to, "Oh, they preach the gospel to those who were unable to hear its message in this life. They are very busy." Although most of us recognize and value the importance of missionary work beyond the veil, we risk taking this blessing for granted. Few of us ever realize that missionary work in the next life is a uniquely LDS belief. Indeed, the grave does hold less darkness for us than for the rest of the world, because we know that our loved ones and countless others can have the opportunity for eternal progression through this great work!

When a young man passes away in what seems to be an untimely fashion, we often say to ourselves that the Lord has a great mission for him. What a joy it is to know that whether the deceased is old or young, male or female, the work that awaits on the other side is full of promise and vigor! Few stories provide so much assurance of this truth as this one:

> One morning at the breakfast table of a good, strong-in-the-gospel family, the youngest son, who was about twenty, said that he had dreamed an extraordinarily vivid dream.
>
> In his dream, he was traveling on a train or bus for some time before he finally reached his destination. Once there, the city was very strange to him. He turned and walked up a street, and as he did so, he noticed several men going into a beautiful building. He joined the crowd and entered in with them. The other men sat down, so he did the same. Soon the meeting was called to order, with a president, assistants, and a clerk seated at the front. He realized that it was an elder's quorum meeting when the clerk called the roll.
>
> The young man listened as ninety-five elders answered the roll call. His name was the ninety-sixth, but when it was called no one answered. The clerk called his name a second time, and still there was silence.
>
> Then the president turned and asked one of the elders why he had failed to have him there at the meeting, and the elder said,
>
> "I did try to have him here but I failed."
>
> The president said, "Be sure to have him here at the next meeting on Wednesday, as that is our last meeting before leaving for our field of labor." After this, the president gave valuable instructions on missionary work.
>
> At this point, the young man awoke and felt impressed to tell his dream to his family at the breakfast table. Lovingly, the boy's mother cau-

tioned him to be very careful in his job as well as on his way to and from work. Of course, he said he would, and when he finished eating, he went down to the store where he was a clerk.

The first customer that came in the store asked for something that was high on the top shelf. The young man hurriedly climbed a ladder, and as he came down with the item he slipped. The fall was fatal. There is no doubt that he answered roll call the next Wednesday at the missionary preparation meeting.[1]

What a comfort it must have been to this young man's mother to have had a witness from her son that he was needed in a great and marvelous work! She was left to rely on her faith about the blessings and covenants he would receive in the next life, just as most of us are usually left to rely on our faith in all respects concerning a seemingly early death. However, sometimes the Lord sees fit to reveal even more concerning the work and mission of those who have been called beyond as related in the following experience:

In January 1898 I left for a mission to Great Britain. On my way I called at the Brigham Young Academy to visit my brother Frank LeSueur. We spent some pleasant hours together, for we loved each other dearly. Just before parting, we held each other's hands and made a covenant that we would follow the Lord's bidding and do anything he desired of us, thus bringing honor to our fa-

---

[1] Bishop LeGrand Richards told this story at the funeral of Ezra Sorensen in the Grace, Idaho Tabernacle. It was recorded in the Yost family memoirs.

ther's name. I was to go into the Jersey and
Guernsey Islands, where our ancestors had come
from, and during my spare time as a missionary, I
would gather genealogical information regarding
them. We discussed this and decided that we
would do our part in the redemption of our dead.
Now I admit that these are rather strange
covenants for two lads — as he was but seven-
teen, and I only nineteen years old — but thus it
was. And then we parted, unaware that we were
never to see one another again in mortality.

After twenty-six months service in the mission field, and after having also secured the pedi-
grees of hundreds of dead in my father's ancestry
over many centuries, I received this cablegram
from the President of the European Mission:

"Released. Outlaws killed Frank. Can you call
Anchonie, Glasgow, Thursday?"

Frank had been called on a mission by the
First Presidency but had not been assigned a field,
and was to leave after my return home. What a
shock this was for me! I had so looked forward to
the few months we would be together after my
mission and before he left, and now our plans
were shattered. For a short time, I felt that being
deprived of his company like this was poor pay
for my diligent service, but then I remembered
having found relief in prayer before. So, I called
on the four elders laboring in Guernsey to kneel
with me in prayer. Each of them prayed for my
comfort and consolation, and then I prayed. After
pleading for the comforting spirit of the Lord, I
asked why my brother had been taken in this
way, and whether or not it was the Lord's will.
After pleading earnestly, I heard a voice from

above which penetrated my very soul. Clear, sweet, and wonderful, it said,

"Your brother is called for a similar purpose as President Woodruff's son."

I recalled immediately how President Woodruff's son, one on whom he had laid a great hope of an eventual earthly career, had been drowned in Idaho. President Woodruff had gone to the temple and asked the Lord why this son was taken, when an angel of the Lord stood before him and asked this question,

"Which of all your sons would you prefer to have charge of the missionary work of preaching the gospel to your kindred in the spirit world?"

President Woodruff spoke the name of the son who was drowned and the angel passed out of his sight.

So then I knew that my brother, Frank, had been called to take charge of the missionary work among my kindred who had passed on. He had been a faithful student at BY Academy and after his return home was called to be a missionary. Therefore he was judged, prepared, and worthy to be the ideal one to take charge of my family's missionary work in the next life. My heart's cries were assuaged and I felt to praise the Lord for I knew of no relative who would fill that important post in a better way. Frank had a wonderful personality, was interested in everyone and a friend of all, especially the downtrodden and weak. He was very sympathetic and had a keen sense of right and duty. This was apparent in his insistence on going to the call of his country when the sheriff asked him to go with a posse after five outlaws. His last words heard by living witnesses a few hours prior to his being am-

bushed and shot down by those outlaws were,
"The sheriff's ahead and will need our help." He
was no deserter and to the last fearlessly did his
duty. Here was a real leader to guide kindred in
the spirit world into the way of salvation. I rejoiced in this knowledge.

When I returned home to Arizona, I had a
feeling I would see him. I sought for this privilege at his grave side but was not favored. A week
or more after my return, my father and I went up
to the sheep camps Frank had been in charge of at
the time of his death. As we drove from camp to
camp, the Mexican herders could talk of nothing
else but Frank and how they liked him. At night
when my father retired under the pines I went a
short distance away, and kneeling in prayer,
asked that I might see Frank and get an idea of
the work he was doing. I felt that my prayer
would be answered.

Returning to the camp bed, I retired, and my
spirit left my body. Looking down, I saw my body
on the bed beside my father. Then I saw a personage standing a few feet from my spirit, dressed
in white and I knew he was my Guardian Angel.
He said,

"Come, go with me."

We passed into space above a great distance,
and then out over the forest, the plain, over hills,
dales, water, cities, and in an incredibly short
time came into a large city which I knew to be a
city where the spirits of those who had passed
away were detained while awaiting preparing for
the resurrection morning. A beautiful city it was,
passing all description with its tall, white buildings, its clean flower-bordered streets, its peace
and loveliness, its perfection. We passed through

the streets with people going here and there and then came before a four-story building which covered an entire block.

"We will go in here, said the angel.

A door opened and a young lady beckoned us to enter. I looked at her wondering who she was, for I did not recall having seen her before. The personage accompanying me said,

"This young lady is a relative of yours, who while living in mortality was killed. She is now assisting in missionary work among your relatives who have died without a knowledge of the gospel, and are assembled to hear the gospel preached."

I looked over the audience, estimating that there were about ten thousand present by comparing the congregation with the assembly at conference time in the Salt Lake Tabernacle. There was a look of expectancy upon their faces as though they were awaiting something to begin just like I have seen at our great conference.

Presently, I heard a person begin speaking and I looked toward the speaker and listened to a sermon on the first principles of the gospel. The speaker explained the principles just as I had heard missionaries present them, excepting baptism, which he said was an earthly covenant that should be attended to while in mortality. However, inasmuch as they had died without being baptized, the ordinance could be attended to for them by proxy, someone living in mortality could take their name and act for them. He explained that there were temples erected upon the earth where kinsmen and friends were being baptized vicariously for the dead; and that if they accepted the baptism and confirmation that was done for them, it would be as valid as if they had attended to it in person while in mortality.[2]

When the speaker had finished he turned around and looked up at me, and I saw that it was my brother, Frank. He looked supremely happy and I felt that I would be willing to go through any sacrifice if I could live to be worthy of such happiness. Then he bowed and smiled at me so joyously that a wonderful thrill passed through me. I shall never forget it.

A young lady was standing beside him, also dressed in white. She bowed and smiled at me in recognition of my visit, and I looked at her very carefully, wondering who she was. The angel said,

"The young lady standing by and assisting your brother is to be his wife."

I looked at her once more, realizing that if I ever saw her again, I would know her.

Then the angel said, "We will pass into the other rooms."

There was a room in which there were many thousands of spirits, arranged in classes with teachers instructing and preparing them with sufficient knowledge to later be instructed like the first group that had seemed so interested and eager to receive the information given to them.

_____

[2]The idea that the first principles of the gospel are taught slightly differently is supported by President Joseph F. Smith's vision of the redemption of the dead (D&C 138:32-34) where he says, "Thus was the gospel preached to those who had died in their sins, without a knowledge of the truth or in transgression, having rejected the prophets. These were taught faith in God, repentance from sin, _vicarious_ baptism for the remission of sins, the gift of the Holy Ghost by the laying on of hands.

And all other principles of the gospel that were necessary for them to know in order to qualify themselves that they might be judged according to men in the flesh, but live according to God in the spirit." (Italics added)

Faithful relatives of mine who had died were in-
structors here, and the listeners, too, were relatives who had died without a knowledge of the
gospel.

After this, we passed into a third hall where
there was confusion and disorder, quarrelling,
and loud talking, and it seemed that force was required to control some of those gathered. There
were also relatives of still darker times, even
darker than the age known as the Dark Ages,
when there was so much sin and wickedness and
ignorance among the inhabitants of the earth.
These required a still more difficult training and
long schooling before they could even come to
the state of the second group, who were willing to
be taught.

Then the angel said, "We will now go back to
your body," and at that we passed out of the
building along the streets of the city, and with the
speed which seemed like lightening over the
great expanse of mountains, plains, seas, and in
almost the speed of light came down into the
mountain camp. I looked around and saw the
sheep bedded a short distance away at the great
pines, my father lying asleep, and my own body
there in bed with no spirit within it. Then I
looked at the angel, standing near. He bowed,
smiled and bid me adieu, and my spirit re-entered my body. I sat up immediately and told my
father of my experience.

Lest you suggest that this was only a dream,
let me give you some proof of the actuality of my
visit beyond.

Patriarch Charles D. Evans, in Provo, Utah,
on the 26th of February, 1896, had promised me
that "The Lord shall give thee the gift of prophecy

thou shall look beyond this world of flesh into the world of spirits and behold its beauty and order and commune with the dead for their redemption" He also went on to say that "At thy hands shall be the power to bind on earth and in heaven."[3] Both these prophecies were fulfilled, for I did in actuality leave my body to visit the spirit world, and I have served in the temples.

At the time of this experience, I knew of no kindred of mine that had been killed, save my brother, and could not identify the young lady at the entrance of the building in the spirit world. However, when I described her to my mother, she said,

"I know who she was. That was Nellie Cdekirk, your cousin who was killed on the fourth of July by being thrown off a horse she was riding. She was acting as the Goddess of Liberty in Vernal, Utah, and her foot caught in the stirrup so that when she was thrown, she did not fall away, but was drug several blocks before the horse could be stopped. When they freed her from the stirrup she was dead. Nellie was the loveliest and best of all of our relatives."

So it was Nellie who was helping Frank and hundreds of other relatives of mine to teach and help our dead kindred come to an understanding of the truth.

And who was the young lady with Frank that the angel said was to become his wife? A few weeks after this manifestation, a Sister Kempe

---

[3]This blessing is recorded in Book A, page 262 of Charles D. Evans' Patriarchal Record. The out-of-body experience fulfills the first promise. Brother LeSueur had been Chairman of the Building Committee of the Arizona Temple and was assistant to the president of the Arizona Temple at the time he bore this testimony.

came from an adjoining town and told my parents that her daughter had died a short time before. On her deathbed she had told her mother that Frank LeSueur had come to visit her in his spirit form and asked her if she would become his wife. She had agreed to do so. Then he told her to tell her mother that she was going to die and that after she did, her mother was to come and ask my parents for consent to having her daughter, Jennie, sealed to Frank. I was called into the consultation, and when I heard it I asked for a photo of the young lady. As soon as I saw it, I recognized the likeness of the young lady with my brother in the spirit world. The sealing was taken care of and those two happy souls are now working together in that most joyous work of soul-saving.[4]

My life has been changed by this experience, for it has been my utmost desire to do all I can for the redemption of my dead, and to help others throughout the church in genealogical and temple work. To me this effort is vital, actual, and without supposition, for I know that the work we are doing for the saving of souls in the spirit world is indeed moving forward. I have seen the great work that is going on in the temples of Utah and Arizona and know from the monthly reports of the work in these temples that I am involved in completing the missionary work being done in

---

[4]The words of Melvin J. Ballard are comforting and supportive of this experience: "Now then, what of your daughters who have died and have not been sealed to some man?. . .The sealing power shall be forever with this Church, and the provisions will be made for them. We cannot run faster than the Lord has provided the way. Their blessing and privileges will come to them in due time. In the mean time, they are safe." *Bryant S. Hinckley, Sermons and Missionary Services of Melvin J. Ballard.*

the spirit prison. To me this is no longer a matter of belief, but a positive knowledge.[5]

From this experience, we can see that the missionary work in the spirit world is not an isolated effort. Groups are organized in families, in elders quorums, to spread the gospel among those who have not heard its message. But are we as mortals without responsibility to do our part? Obviously the answer is no. Those who have gone beyond can carry the truth to our ancestors who have not yet received it, but we must do the work for them, so that their acceptance of the gospel can be of effect. President Ezra Taft Benson has taught that,

> It is not sufficient for a husband and wife to be sealed in the temple...they must also be eternally linked with their progenitors and see that the work is done for those ancestors.[6]

Progression is not something we do alone. When we carefully consider President Benson's words in relationship to the following statement of President Spencer W. Kimball's we cannot fail to see the active, vital way our individual salvation is linked with that of our extended family:

> Through the priesthood's new and everlasting covenant of marriage, all the elect children of God who are gathered together out of the earth

---

[5]James A. LeSueur, "A Peep into the Spirit World," (mimeographed mss.).

[6]Ezra Taft Benson, Regional Representatives' seminar, Apr. 3, 1981.

may be sealed together in family units...into the organized, eternal family of God.[7]

That we may each be included with those we love in that Celestial Family, let us come to share Joseph F. Smith's enthusiasm when he stated, "There isn't anything so great and so glorious in this world as to labor for the salvation of the living and for the redemption of the dead."[8]

---

[7]Spencer W. Kimball, "The Things of Eternity--Stand We in Jeopardy?" *Ensign,* Jan. 1977, p. 4.

[8]Joseph F. Smith, *Young Women's Journal,* Mar. 1912, p. 130.

Questions and Answers

1. Why is missionary work the greatest work in the spirit world?

The Lord declared through the Prophet Joseph Smith that all people would be given the opportunity to hear the gospel preached, and He made no distinction between the living and the dead:

> For verily the voice of the Lord is unto all men, and there is none to escape; and there is no eye that shall not see, neither ear that shall not hear, neither heart that shall not be penetrated. (D&C 1:2)

Concerning this, Elder Bruce R. McConkie of the Council of the Twelve Apostles explained that "The great work in the world of the spirits is the preaching of the gospel to those who are imprisoned by sin and false traditions."[9]

When we consider the vast numbers of people who have lived upon this earth without the fullness of the gospel, there is very little room for debate or rationalization as to what many of those spirits dedicated to serving God will be doing in the next life. President Brigham Young taught:

---

[9]McConkie, *Mormon Doctrine*, p. 762.

What are they doing there? They are preaching, preaching all the time, and preparing the way for us to hasten our work. . . .[10]

Although there are other types of work in the spirit world, there appears to be none more important or of a broader scope than the preaching of the gospel.

2. *Who has the responsibility to do missionary work in the spirit world?*

In his vision of the redemption of the dead, Joseph F. Smith saw the righteous spirits, those who had been faithful in the testimony of Jesus while in the flesh, in the spirit world. He saw that the Savior organized His forces among them and appointed messengers, clothed with power and authority, and sent them forth to preach the gospel to the captives who were bound but would repent of their sins and receive the gospel. (see D&C 138)

President Brigham Young said:

The faithful Elders who leave this world will preach to the spirits in the spirit world...there are millions and millions to every Elder who leaves here, and yet every spirit will be preached to that has had a tabernacle here on earth and become accountable...When the faithful Elders, holding this Priesthood, go into the spirit world they carry with them the same power and priesthood that they had while in the mortal tabernacle. They have got the victory over the power of the enemy

---

[10]Brigham Young, *Journal of Discourses*, Vol. 3, pp. 370, 372.

here, consequently when they leave this world
they have perfect control over those evil spirits,
and they cannot be buffeted by Satan.[11]

Parley P. Pratt echoed the same doctrine, saying
that if a man died, having magnified his priesthood, it could not be taken from him and would
remain with him in the world of spirits. When
such a man has died, Elder Pratt explained:

> If he can find a person worthy of salva-
> tion...he remembers what he may teach and...he
> discovers that he has got a mission, and that mis-
> sion is to those souls who had not the privilege
> which we have in this world, that they may be
> partakers of the Gospel as well as we.[12]

And referring to the Elders of Israel, President
Wilford Woodruff taught:

> The Lord hath need of some on the other side
> of the veil. He reserves some to labor here, and
> he takes whom he will...If we tarry here He ex-
> pects us to labor in the cause of salvation and if
> we go hence, we expect to continue our
> work...The only difference is, while we are here
> we are subject to pain and sorrow, while they on
> the other side are free from affliction of every
> kind.[13]

---

[11]Brigham Young, *Journal of Discourses*, Vol. 3, p. 371.

[12]Burton, *For They Shall Be Comforted*, pp. 76-77.

[13]Wilford Woodruff, *Journal of Discourses*, Vol. 22, pp. 333-334.

These brethren leave little question about the nature of the priesthood and its eternal responsibility to spread the gospel. Although women do not hold the priesthood, Joseph F. Smith referred to sisters who have been set apart to administer sacred temple ordinances when he explained:

> Who is going to carry the testimony of Jesus Christ to the hearts of the women who have passed away without a knowledge of the gospel? Well, to my mind, it is a simple thing. These good sisters have been set apart, ordained to the work, called to it, authorized by the authority of the Holy Priesthood to minister for their sex, in the house of God for the living and for the dead, will be fully authorized and empowered to preach the gospel and minister to the women while the elders and prophets are preaching it to the men. The things we experience here are typical of the things of God and the life beyond us.[14]

3. *How is missionary work done in the spirit world?*

Organization and Authority

It appears that missionary work in the spirit world is organized according to the same pattern as that followed here on earth. Elder Parley P. Pratt taught that those holding the keys of priesthood power would proclaim the gospel "after the pattern of Jesus Christ," He went on to indicate that the spirits of everyone else would have the gospel

---

[14]Joseph F. Smith, *Young Women's Journal*, Vol. 23, p. 130.

taught to them either in mortality or in the spirit
world under the direction of priesthood authority.

Individual or Group Teaching

Although the usual approach to teaching the
gospel in mortality is to focus on individuals and
families, there appears to be some variation from
this in the spirit world. In James W. Lesueur's experience, we read of the gospel being preached to
congregations on three different levels.

David Lynn Brooks was visited by his deceased
wife and also saw groups of people being taught the
gospel:

> ...she invited me to look into the spirit world,
> and asked what I could see. I told her I could see a
> group of people seated in a room or hall at a table
> or at desks with note pads and pencils. She then
> asked, "Do you know who these people are?" I
> told her I didn't recognize any of them. She asked
> me if I remembered the people we had done the
> temple work for in 1929 and 1930. She and I had
> worked the entire winter gathering genealogy of
> her people and then we did the temple work for
> them. She then told me that she had been called
> by the Priesthood to teach the gospel to those
> people and that she was very happy doing that
> work.[15]

John Peterson also describes the gospel being
taught in a group setting:

---

[15]David Lynn Brooks, *Personal Records of David Lynn Brooks*, as cited in
Crowther, *Life Everlasting*, pp. 59-60 (italics added).

> The elder apostle stood up in the stand and said to the people, "Stop right there!" Then he sat down and perfect stillness prevailed when the young apostle rose up to preach to the congregation...he spoke at some length...then took his seat, when the elder apostle arose and told the people they could now retire, which they did, some of them in as noisy and boisterous manner, so that I thought they were as disorderly in the spirit world as here.[16]

One last example is Ella Jensen's experience that we have already discussed, in which she described a long room filled with hundreds of small children arranged in a sort of Primary or Sunday School and presided over by Eliza R. Snow.

Reports like these leave no doubt that the gospel may be taught to larger groups in the spirit world than in mortality.

4. *How successful is missionary work in the spirit world?*

The Prophet Joseph Smith taught that God made provision for *every* spirit to be saved unless he had committed the unpardonable sin of denying the Holy Ghost. He said:

> If a man has knowledge, he can be saved, although, if he has been guilty of great sins, he will be punished for them. But when he consents to

---

[16]Peterson, "Was Dead and Came to Life Again." *Millennial Star*, 1916, pp. 699-700 (italics added).

obey the gospel, whether here or in the world of spirits, he is saved.[17]

And President Lorenzo Snow explained further:

When the gospel is preached to the spirits in prison, the success attending that preaching will be far greater than that attending the preaching of our elders in this life. I believe there will be very few indeed of those spirits who will not gladly receive the gospel when it is carried to them. The circumstances there will be a thousand times more favorable.[18]

---

[17]Burton, *For They Shall Be Comforted*, p. 72.

[18]Lorenzo Snow as quoted by Burton, *For They Shall Be Comforted*, p. 50.

8

Genealogical And Temple Work

Peter E. Johnson was called on a mission in 1898, and, at the last minute, his area of service was changed from East Kentucky to Mississippi. In less than six weeks he was struck with malaria, but was prevented from being sent home by a yellow fever quarantine. He related:

> I was lying on a bed, burning up with the fever, and the elders who had been sent to ascertain my condition were very much alarmed. They stepped out of the room and held whispered consultations. They were so far away that under ordinary conditions I could not have heard what was said; but in some manner my hearing was made so keen that I heard their conversation as well as if they had been at my bedside. They said it was impossible to think of my recovering, and that I never would go home unless I went in a box. They therefore decided they might just as

well notify the president and make necessary arrangements.

The following day I asked to be removed into the hall, where it was cooler. I was lying on a pallet (or bed). There was an attendant with me; the others having gone to Sunday School, which was being held about one hundred yards away. Soon after they had left I was, apparently, in a dying condition, and my attendant became so fearful of my appearance and condition that he left me. I desired a drink of water but of course was unable to get it myself. I became discouraged, and wondered why it was that I was sent to Mississippi and whether it was simply to die in the field. I felt that I would prefer death, rather than live and endure the fever and the agony through which I was passing.

I thought of my people at home and of the conditions then surrounding me, and decided that I might just as well pass from this life. Just as I reached that conclusion this thought came to me: "You will not die unless you choose death." This was a new thought, and I hesitated to consider the question; then I made the choice that I would rather die.

Soon after that, my spirit left the body; just how I cannot tell. But I perceived myself standing some four or five feet in the air, and saw my body lying on the bed. I felt perfectly natural, but as this was a new condition I began to make observations. I turned my head, shrugged my shoulders, felt with my hands, and realized that it was I myself. I also knew that my body was lying, lifeless, on the bed. While I was in a new environment, it did not seem strange, for I realized everything that was going on, and perceived that

I was the same in the spirit as I had been in the body. While contemplating this new condition, something attracted my attention, and on turning around I beheld a personage, who said,

"You did not know that I was here."

I replied, "No, but I see you are. Who are you?"

"I am your guardian angel; I have been following you constantly while on earth."

"What will you do now?"

"I am to report on your presence, and you will remain here until I return."

He informed me, on returning, that we should wait there, as my sister desired to see me, but was busy just at that time. Presently she came. She was glad to see me and asked if I was offended because she kept me waiting. She explained that she was doing some work that she wished to finish.

Just before my eldest sister died she asked me to enter into this agreement: That if she died first, she was to watch over me, protect me from those who might seek my downfall, and that she would be the first to meet me after death. If I happened to die first, she wished me to do the same for her. We made this agreement, and this was the reason that my sister was the first one of my relatives to meet me. After she arrived, my mother and other sisters and friends came to see me, and we discussed various topics, as we would do here on meeting friends. After we had spent some little time in conversation, the guide came to me with a message that I was wanted by some of the apostles who had lived on the earth in this dispensation. As soon as I came into their presence, I was asked if I desired to remain there. This seemed very strange, for it had never occurred to me that we would have any choice there in the spirit world, as to whether we should remain or return to the earth life. I was asked if I felt satisfied with conditions there. I informed them that I was, and had no desire to return to the fever and misery from which I had been suffering while in the body. After some little conversation this question was repeated, with the same answer.

Then I asked, "If I remain, what will I be asked to do?"

I was informed that I would preach the gospel to the spirits there, as I had been preaching it to the people here and that I would do so under the immediate direction of the Prophet Joseph. This remark brought to my mind a question which has been much discussed here, as to whether or not the Prophet Joseph Smith is a resurrected being. While I did not ask the question, they read it in my mind, and immediately said,

"You wish to know whether the prophet has his body or not?"

"Yes, I would like to know."

I was told that the Prophet Joseph has his body, as also his brother Hyrum, and that as soon as I could do more with my body than I could do without it, my body would be resurrected. I was again asked if I still desired to remain. This bothered me considerably, for I had already expressed myself as being satisfied. I inquired why it was that I was asked so often if I was satisfied and if I desired to remain: I was then informed that my progenitors had made a request that if I chose I might be granted the privilege of returning, to again take up my mortal body, in order that I might gather my father's genealogy and do the necessary work in the temple for my ancestors. As I was still undecided, one of the apostles said,

"We will now show you what will take place if you remain here in the spirit world; after which you can decide."

When we returned to the place where my body was lying, I was informed with emphasis that my first duty would be to watch the body until after it had been disposed of, as that was necessary knowledge for me to have in the resurrection.

I then saw the elders send a message to President Rich, at Chattanooga, and in due time all preparations were made for the shipment of my body to Utah. One thing seemed peculiar to me, that I was able to read the telegram as it ran along the wires, as easily as I could read the pages of a book. I could see President Rich, when he received the telegram in Chattanooga. He walked the floor, wringing his hands with the thought in his mind: "How can I send a message to his father?"

The message was finally sent, and I could follow it on the wire. I saw the station and the telegraph operator at Price, Utah. I heard the instrument click as the message was received, and saw the operator write out the message and send it by phone from Price to Huntington. I also saw clearly the Huntington office and the man who received the message. I could see clearly and distinctly the people on the street. I did not have to hear what was said, for I was able to read their thoughts from their countenances. The message was delivered to my aunt who went out with others to find my father. In due time he received the message. He did not seem to be overcome by

4. What effects do near death experiences have on people's lives?

In many of the experiences we have shared thus far, comments have been made like, "It was a life-changing experience," or, "I have tried to do [such and such] differently." We have read about strengthened testimonies of the gospel and increased love for the Savior, and of new attitudes toward both life and death. In general, most people who have died place more value on two things than they did before: 1) Cultivating a deeper love for others, and 2) Acquiring knowledge.[14]

---

[14]Dr. Moody noticed the same results (*Life After Life*, pp. 88-96) and he emphasized that although every person who had such an experience was no longer afraid to die, all of them would reject suicide as a means of returning to the spirit world.

the news, but began to make preparations to meet the body. I then saw my father at the railroad station in Price, waiting for my body to arrive. Apparently, he was unaffected; but when he heard the whistle of the train which was carrying my body, he went behind the depot and cried as if his heart would break.

While I had been accompanying the body enroute, I was still able to see what was going on at home. The distance, apparently, did not affect my vision. As the train approached the station I went to my father's side, and seeing his great anguish, I informed my companion that I would return. He expressed his approval of my decision and said he was pleased with the choice I had made.

By some spiritual power, all these things had been shown to me as they would occur if I did not return to the body. Immediately upon making this choice or decision, my companion said:

"Good. Your progenitors will be pleased with your decision."

I asked the question why, and I was told that it was their desire that I should return to the body, hunt up my father's genealogies and do their work in the temple.

Just how my spirit entered my body I cannot tell, but I saw the apostle place his hands upon the head of my prostrate body, and almost instantly I realized that the change had come and I was again in the body. The first thing that I knew, I felt a warm life-giving spot on the crown of my head, which passed through my entire body, going out to the tips of my fingers and toes. . . .[1]

---

[1] Peter E. Johnson, "A Testimony," *The Relief Society Magazine*, Vol. VII, No. 8, August, 1920.

Peter Johnson further explains that the local elder who had been left to watch him had become frightened at his condition and had gone to Sunday School, notifying the others of Peter's death at the end of the services. The elders, Saints, and his friends had gathered outside the fence trying to decide what to do, when suddenly Peter came out of the house in search of a cool drink of water. Those who were gathered around were frightened, thinking he was a spirit, but once he assured them, they all rejoiced.

One noteworthy aspect of Peter's story is the importance attached to his ancestor's request that he do their genealogy and temple work. Yet, in spite of their wishes he was granted his free agency. Thus it is with each of us. The Lord has a plan in mind and we each have callings and responsibilities associated with that plan, but we each have the ability to choose what we will do. Like Peter, we have our own choice regarding our involvement in genealogy and temple work.

Section 2 of the Doctrine and Covenants explains the purpose of genealogy and temple work:

> Behold, I will reveal unto you the Priesthood, by the hand of Elijah the prophet, before the coming of the great and dreadful day of the Lord.
>
> And he shall plant in the hearts of the children the promises made to the fathers, and the hearts of the children shall turn to their fathers.
>
> It it were not so, the whole earth would be utterly wasted at his coming.

In spite of our familiarity with this revelation and perhaps because of it, we may need to consider these words of Joseph F. Smith's before we truly understand our responsibility:

> Why would the earth be wasted? Simply because if there is not a welding link between the fathers and the children — which is the work for the dead — then we will all stand rejected.[2]

When we realize the importance of our relationship to our family, we can better understand Sister Southgate's anxiety as described by Brother Carr:

> In the block where I lived was a family by the name of Southgate. They were an average family who worked hard to support seven children. Every day I went to the Southgate home to play with their children or they were at our home. I also saw them faithfully at church every Sunday.
> One day Sister Southgate discovered that she had a lump in her breast, so they drove by team to Provo and she had both breasts removed. But the cancer had spread and nothing more could be done for her. There were no drugs in those days to relieve the pain, which was constantly with her. The bishopric administered to her many times, but only temporary relief was obtained. The membership of the ward called a fast on her behalf, and prayed for her. They asked the Lord to let her pass on, that they could not stand to see Sister Southgate suffer any longer.

---

[2]Joseph Fielding Smith, *Doctrines of Salvation*, 2:122.

After the fasting and prayer meeting, Sister Southgate died. They had no mortuary in those days. A homemade casket was made, and the Relief Society dressed Sister Southgate for burial. The funeral services were arranged, and her body was placed carefully in a casket.

Just prior to the time of the services and when a number of people were present, they heard Sister Southgate call out from where she lay in the casket. She asked her husband then if he were sure that she had been sealed to her parents. She said there was something wrong, as her mother and father and other members of her family were together, but she did not seem to belong to them.

Her husband got out the family record and found that his wife's family had gone to the St. George Temple years before, and had been sealed. An elderly lady who had traveled to the community for the funeral remembered that when the Southgate family had gone to the St. George Temple to have their family sealed, there was an epidemic of measles among the children and perhaps Sister Southgate had not been able to go with the others. Sister Southgate later wrote to the temple for information, and when she received an answer she found that all her family except herself were listed on the temple sealing.

She discussed her experiences in the spirit world with the many friends and relatives that had gathered for her funeral. She had visited with many who had departed this life and she told of schools for children who had died, and of the peaceful conditions of paradise. While she was there, some messengers had asked her to return and finish her work in mortality. She explained that she told them she had suffered terribly for many months, and could not bear to go back and endure the pain. They told her that Satan had such great power on the earth that her children needed their mother to build strong faith. They promised her that because she had not complained of her suffering, nor had bitterness in her heart, she would never have to suffer mortal pain again.

Sister Southgate had good health from then on. She had been unable to raise her arm, but after that she could hold it high above her head. She was sealed in the temple to her family and lived to see all her children married in the temple for time and for eternity. Her children remained true in the faith and valiant in helping build up the kingdom of God on the earth.

When Sister Southgate was threescore and ten she asked her husband if he would feel very lonesome if she were to pass over. He answered that he would, but perhaps he would be called over first. The next morning Brother Southgate found that his wife had gone over to her beloved parents, and without struggle or pain. She had just gone to sleep.[3]

How could we suppose that our ancestors feel any less strongly about being sealed into their own patriarchal lines and having an opportunity for progression than Sister Southgate did? Audrey, who tells us the following story, cannot. Before she was even a member of the church or had any

---

[3]This is the record of Brother Carr's testimony, as given in the Arizona temple, and recorded in the Yost Memoirs.

inkling of the importance of genealogical work, her ancestors were striving to impress the need for it upon her:

> I was born in 1894 in Pennsylvania. While I was a baby, my parents attended a small Methodist church. It was a small, frame building painted white and containing just one large room and two small rooms off the vestry. When I was between the ages of three and five, I had a peculiar dream. It seems strange now to think of it happening to such a small child, but it did.
>
> I thought I was out in front of the little church looking at the belfry because my four grandparents were there, one in each of the windows. I stopped under one grandfather's window and called up to him, "What are you doing up there, and why don't you go on to heaven where you belong?"
>
> He turned just a bit and looked down at me and said, "Child, we can't go on until you do some work for us."
>
> I had this dream over and over again all night, and it made a very strong impression on my mind. The next morning, I asked my father, "What can we do for dead people?"
>
> "I don't know," he said. "As far as I know, you can't do anything for anyone after they're dead. If you want to do something for someone, you had better do it while they are alive." Then he looked at me very strangely and said, "Why did you ask such a question, Audrey? You have always asked odd questions, but this one beats them all."
>
> I told him about my dream and he said, "I don't see how you could dream of my parents, since they died before you were born."

Well, I didn't know either, but I was sure it was them.

Sometime later I went with my mother to my family reunion. While we were there, I got terribly sick, and someone put a blanket on a bench not far from the table so that I could see all that was going on. My mother's uncle, Hezekiah the lawyer, gave a talk about the genealogy of the family. There were some beautiful swings in that park, but the Lord must have wanted me to hear Uncle Kai's talk because I learned many things about my family.

When I was twenty-five, I developed abscesses in my intestines. I had been through several operations and was in a Seventh Day Adventist Hospital when I died.

When it happened, the first thing I saw was a light all around me. It was so bright that at first I couldn't see beyond the light, but my eyes finally got used to it. My first thought was for my two daughters ages five and seven. I wanted to talk to my parents. They were beside my body, yet they were so far away. I tried to talk to them, but it was impossible.

I didn't see anything, but this voice came from the light. He knew that I was worried about my little girls and told me that I could go back if I would do the work my Heavenly Father had for me to do. I agreed, and instantly I was alive again.

I didn't get better right away, but I was not worried. The doctor couldn't understand why I was so calm, especially since I had to have another operation. I knew I would live, but I was afraid to tell anyone about my experience of dying. I just kept all this to myself.

As soon as I was well enough to get in the car, I asked my husband to take me to visit all the religions in San Diego where we lived. We contacted everyone, even the Holy Rollers. Six months later, LDS missionaries knocked at my door. An elder gave me a pamphlet with the Salt Lake Temple in the upper right-hand corner. I wanted to ask him a question, but he was nervous.

"It's my first day tracting, and I'd better fetch my companion from around the corner if you really want to ask a question," he said.

"But this is a very easy question," I said, trying to keep him from going. I pointed to the pamphlet and said, "What do you use this building for?"

"We do work for the living and the dead in there," he said, and I went gooseflesh all over. I knew at that moment that that was why my life had been spared.

At the time I was seeing the missionaries, I was a member of the Quaker Church. I liked their church, but it was missing the one thing I was seeking for — work for the dead. Then I got pneumonia, and again no one thought I would live. The Quakers held a prayer meeting for me one morning, and by 10:00 a.m. I was sitting up eating lunch. When the elders found me in the hospital, I told them how I had been healed.

One missionary said to his companion, "How do you account for that?" (supposing that since the Quakers didn't have any authority there must be something wrong).

His partner treated it very flippantly, saying, "Sometimes things like that just happen."

I lost interest in the missionaries right away since I thought they didn't realize the power of prayer. It was nine years before I joined the Church, and we moved to Wisconsin right after that. But all during those nine years I kept having this dream, sometimes every night, sometimes once a week.

I would be asleep, and, all of a sudden, I would jump out of bed because I heard this voice saying, "You promised to do something, but you didn't!" I always looked around, but there was never anybody there. So, I would just get back in bed and go to sleep.

Now the dream went on after we joined the Church, and finally I went to my doctor and told him about it because I thought I must be going crazy. He said that after I went to Salt Lake City and did the work I was supposed to do, the dreams would stop. Well, I did and the dreams stopped. My relatives must have wanted me to do that work in a really bad way.

Clearly, deceased spirits put great importance on genealogy work, yet each of us knows that this is no simple task. In fact, sometimes the magnitude of it is positively overwhelming. Elder Boyd K. Packer felt this way, until one day while he was pondering the matter, he came to the realization that there is something each of us can do for all those who have died. "I came to see that any one of us by himself, can care about them, all of them, and love them." For Elder Packer, this was a great inspiration, because then he realized that there was a starting point in this great work.[4]

Pat found that such a realization can come to each of us when we immerse ourselves in service for those who have preceded us into the next world:

> In August of 1977, my family and I made a long-planned excursion into northern Arkansas to visit an old graveyard, now hidden in a national forest. Some of my family are buried in that cemetery, and I needed some tombstone dates to complete part of the genealogy work I had been doing.
>
> We bounced along the narrow, rutted forest road, overhanging limbs scraping our station wagon and heavy dust billowing up about us. A local resident had given us directions but soon we realized that we were lost. We stopped to pray for guidance and started off again. Finally we pulled into a shaded clearing and saw an old, abandoned church house and cemetery.
>
> Eagerly, my wife and I got out and approached the graveyard, notebooks and pens in hand. Family names, like old, familiar friends greeted us as we pulled back weeds and uprighted tombstones searching for names and dates. It was hard, tiring work fighting the briars and deciphering the traces of what had survived the wind and rain of lifetimes. At last we felt we had found all the information possible, and my wife headed back for the car. I still felt that there was some-

---

[4]Boyd K. Packer, *The Holy Temple*, Salt Lake City, Ut.: Bookcraft Inc., 1980, pp. 238-239.

thing else to be done, and my attention was drawn to the old church. Feeling impressed to enter it, I climbed the steps, opened the only door, and peered in.

It was a one-room chapel, still filled with old, handhewn pews. Closing the door, I walked quietly up to the front. I knelt and thanked my Heavenly Father for His help, and for a few brief glorious moments, as I knelt, I could actually see the people there, filling the little church. Some were standing and others sat in the pews. All were clothed in the simple country dress of their time. Some of the men had beards or moustaches and two women held infants in their arms. They had gathered and waited for me in that little church where most of them had worshipped in mortality. Although a few appeared indifferent, most of them were smiling happily.

A strong feeling of peace and joy overcame me, almost unbearable in its sweet intensity. I bowed my head humbly, as grateful tears fell from my cheeks. I felt a part of that glorious eternity, an accepted part of my own family. Though we had never met before, they knew me and I knew them. No longer were they just names or dates. After a while I lifted my head and they were gone.

As I rejoined my wife, I knew more strongly than ever before that our progenitors wanted their work done. And I know that our loving Father would have us all unite our families across the chasm of death with the saving bridge of genealogical research and temple sealings.[5]

---

[5]Pat gave permission for use of this story entitled, "In An Old Country Church," which is also recounted in the *Ensign*, April, 1983, p. 29.

After hearing testimonies like these, we cannot doubt Joseph Smith's words when he said that "the greatest responsibility in this world that God has laid upon us is to seek after our dead," and that "those Saints who neglect it in behalf of their deceased relatives, do it at the peril of their own salvation."[6] With this in mind, these words of President Ezra Taft Benson should hold great meaning for us:

> The need for each of us to perform temple and genealogical work has never been more urgent. We must redouble our efforts to accomplish this great and holy work. We cannot hope for perfection without being linked to our forefathers. Neither can they hope for perfection without us. My brothers and sisters, it is up to each of us to see that this work is done."[7]

---

[6]Joseph Smith, Jr., *History of the Church*, 6:313 and 4:426.

[7]Ezra Taft Benson, Regional Representatives' seminar, Apr. 3, 1981, p. 2.

Questions and Answers

1. *What is the rationale for doing ordinance work for the dead?*

The answer to this question is clearly set forth in all the Standard Works, so we will only provide a quick review of some important points.

While teaching the Corinthian saints about the reality of the resurrection, the Apostle Paul pointed to their continued practice of baptism for the dead as proof of the resurrection's reality:

> Else what shall they do which are baptized for the dead, if the dead rise not at all? why are they then baptized for the dead? (I Cor. 15:29)

Furthermore, in a revelation given to the Prophet Joseph Smith, the Lord indicated that the saints were to build a temple where baptisms for the dead could be performed.[8] He promised that such ordinances, if they were properly attended to in the temple in the presence of a recorder and witnesses with the necessary keys and authority, would be binding on earth and in heaven.[9]

We can also turn to experiences with the spirit world to find overwhelming support for the need for vicarious ordinance work. In speaking of our

---

[8] In D&C 124:29.

[9] In D&C 127:5-7. Also see D&C 128.

relationship to this responsibility, President Spencer W. Kimball said:

> He provided the opportunity whereby they might repent of their sins, change their attitudes and their lives, and live according to God in the spirit. We do not know how many millions of spirits are involved. We know that many have passed away in wars, pestilence, and in various accidents. We know that the spirit world is filled with the spirits of men who are waiting for you and me to get busy — waiting as the signers of the Declaration of Independence waited. "Why," they asked President Wilford Woodruff, "why do you keep us waiting?" That question continues to be asked of us also by our own people.
>
> Some of us have had occasion to wait for someone or something for a minute, an hour, a day, a week, or even a year. Can you imagine how our progenitors must feel, some of whom have perhaps been waiting for decades and even centuries for the temple work to be done for them?[10]

2. *Is ordinance work ever initiated by disembodied spirits?*

It seems that this practice does occur. There are few individuals busy with genealogy and temple work who have not felt some impressions, dreams, visitations, or other types of spiritual experiences regarding their efforts in behalf of departed relatives. Each of the experiences shared in this chapter

---

[10]Spencer W. Kimball, "The Things of Eternity--Stand We in Jeopardy?" *Ensign*, Jan. 1977, pp. 5-6.

illustrate the nearness of those waiting for us to do their work. Their eagerness is clear in these words of Wilford Woodruff at the dedication of the Salt Lake Temple:

> If the veil could be taken from our eyes and we could see into the spirit world, we would see that Joseph Smith, Brigham Young, and John Taylor had gathered together every spirit that ever dwelt in the flesh in this church since its organization. We would also see the faithful apostles and elders of the Nephites who dwelt in the flesh in the days of Jesus Christ. In that assembly we would also see Isaiah and every prophet and apostle that ever prophesied of the great work of God.
>
> In the midst of these spirits we would see the Son of God, the Savior, who presides and guides and controls the preparing of the kingdom of God on earth and in heaven...From that body of spirits, when we shout "Hosannah to God and the Lamb!" there is a mighty shout goes up of "Glory to God in the Highest!" that the God of Israel has permitted His people to finish this temple and prepare it for the great work that lies before the Latter-day Saints.[11]

But spirit beings are not only present at various assemblies such as the dedication of temples. Many people involved in genealogy work have experienced some sort of prodding or stimulation to get on with their work. This is one experience:

---

[11]Wilford Woodruff as quoted by Burton, p. 422.

One night...I awakened from a deep sleep by a voice which came to my mind. As I listened to what was being said, I realized that my great-great-grandfather was speaking to me. I lay there for a moment listening and thinking. My great-great-grandfather was telling me to have his family sealed to him.

At first, I thought I must be imagining things, and I lay there and thought about my great-great-grandparents. I decided I should do their genealogy and would get to it when I had the time. Then I began to doze. I was startled when the voice returned and said much the same thing, only this time urging me to have the work done *soon*. I decided to do something about it the next day. Apparently, however, my grandfather knew I would probably be distracted the next day, because he spoke to me yet a third time, and told me to do something NOW!

I could not quite believe what was happening, but in the middle of the night I got up and began working on my genealogy.

Eventually, I was able to go to the temple with my cousin and have my great-great-grandparents sealed. I can testify that I felt their presence there in the temple and knew that, at last, they could be truly happy and together eternally.[12]

There are also accounts of spirits' involvement in providing information for ordinance work. Anthon H. Lund, president of the Manti Temple from 1891-1893, said:

---

[12]Terry Lynn Fisher, "Please Do My Work," *Ensign*. Aug. 1983, pp. 54-55.

I remember one day...a brother from Mount Pleasant rode down to the temple to take part in the work, and as he passed the cemetery in Ephraim, he looked ahead (it was early in the morning), and there was a large multitude all dressed in white, and he wondered how that could be. Why should there be so many up here; it was too early for a funeral, he thought; but as he drove up several of them stepped to the front of him...They said, "Are you going to the temple?" "Yes." "Well these that you see here are your relatives and they want you to do work for them." "Yes," he said, "but I am going down today to finish my work. I have no more names and I do not know the names of those who say they are related to me." "But when you go down to the temple today you will find there are records that give our names." He was surprised. He looked until they all disappeared, and drove on.

As he came into the temple, Recorder Farnsworth came up to him and said, "I have just received records from England and they all belong to you." There were hundreds of names that had just arrived, and what was told him by these persons that he saw was fulfilled. You can imagine what joy came to his heart, and what a testimony it was to him that the Lord wants His work done.[13]

Sometimes departed spirits are even more directly involved in temple work. John M. Lang, who was an ordinance worker in the St. George Temple,

---

[13]N.B. Lundwall, *Temples of the Most High*, 10th ed., Salt Lake City, Ut.: Bookcraft Inc., 1941, p. 124.

wrote the following description of what he saw. Although this experience should not be generalized nor considered official Church doctrine, it certainly is a probable description of the way the work is carried forth:

> One day while baptismal rites were being performed, I distinctly heard a voice at the east end of the font, very close to the ceiling, calling the names of the dead to witness their own baptism, allowing a moment for each spirit to present itself. After hearing many names called, I noticed a difference in the pronunciation of some of them. It seemed that the spirit who was calling must have a different list than ours...I was so impressed at the time that I placed my arm about the shoulders of Brother W. T. Morris, clerk, but it was not discernable to him. . . .
>
> This occurrence had taken place in March of 1928, and it continued to prey upon my mind for some months, until one day in October I had gone to an upper room of the Temple as was my custom, to offer secret prayer, asking for the assistance of God in my work, and to thank Him for showing me that there was a recording angel in His house, to keep a perfect record of that which transpired. I had finished my prayer and was about to leave the room when the question flashed through my mind, "But where and how does He get these names? Some of them were not pronounced the same as ours."
>
> . . . God knew my thoughts; I never asked of Him to know. The explanation came to me in these words: "Every spirit that comes to earth has a guardian angel, whose duty it is to keep a record of the individual's life parentage, the conditions

under which it was born, its inheritance, environment, thoughts and desires, and when the individual's life is completed, the guardian angel's
mission ends. It returns, makes its report and
hands in the record it has kept. This record is
placed upon the other book, spoken of as the
Book of Life."[14]

You remember Eliza Neville's visit with her father, where she saw her family standing with their
backs toward one another and he said that they
were complaining about paying their tithing,
though it was used for building temples. "If they
could only see!" he lamented, and then the following scene unfolded:

(She saw) myriads of people reaching out just
as far as her eyes could see, and her father said,
"They couldn't walk through two or three temples on earth in a century's time, much less do
the work which must be done. Now, Eliza, I put
this responsibility on you to see that my family is
united and working in harmony with the
church."[15]

3. *How do we know if the genealogy and temple
work we do is accurate, sufficient, and accepted
by those we do it for?*

The most likely answer to this question is simply through revelation, or through contact from the
spirit who has departed. However, Elder Melvin J.

---

[14]Crowther, *Life Everlasting*, p. 138-139.

[15]Crowther, *Life Everlasting*, p. 111.

Ballard has provided both encouragement and increased understanding in these words:

> The dead know where their records are, so you are to search until you have gone as far as you can. But of course, there are hosts of men and women in the spirit world whose records don't exist anywhere on the earth, but whose record is in the spirit world...When you have done all you can do and have reached the limit what will happen? As always in the past, man's extremity is God's opportunity... When we have done our utmost, then will come the day when the authorities that preside on the other side will come and make known all who have received the gospel in the spirit world and everyone entitled to have their work done. That is the simplest thing in the world. When the Lord is ready, it will be very simple and very easy. We can speed that day by doing now the work that we can do.[16]

Based on the experiences in this chapter and innumerable others, departed spirits play a very active role in genealogy work and in subsequent temple ordinance work. Their role may be merely to impress on our minds the importance of the task, or to reveal that some unfinished ordinance work needs to be completed, or even give specific requests for work to be done. Beyond this, they also keep up a separate recording system keeping track of the ordinances performed for those who are in the spirit world.

---

[16]See *Utah Genealogical and Historical Magazine*, Vol. 23:148-149.

9

Progression Toward Perfection

There is a very old Christian idea that the next world is Purgatory, an in-between place where we suffer to pay for the sins of our mortal life before we can go to heaven. Like many other beliefs common to the Christian world, this notion holds a reflection of the truth. Through latter-day revelation we have come to understand that we do, indeed, take our habits and inclinations with us when we pass through the veil, and must strive to overcome them there.[1] We also know that, although the time we spend in the spirit world is like a second chance to hear the gospel and improve ourselves, overcoming our weaknesses is much more difficult after we have been separated from our bodies.[2] Latter-day Saints generally think of this ongoing struggle to-

---

[1]See question #3 in Chapter 3.

[2]Refer to question #3 in Chapter 3, especially Melvin J. Ballard's remarks.

ward perfection more in terms of progression than penitence.

In the following account we should be encouraged in knowing that we can continue to improve ourselves before the final judgment, but also warned to use the opportunities of this life to grow as much as we possibly can, keeping in perspective that it is a test of limited duration:

> A few months before my wife, Maybeth, passed away, we talked about our past life together, considering those things we had done well, but also thinking about our failures. The dominant theme that brought us the most sorrow was our lack of success with our children. We felt we had failed to get them to live as useful, Christian lives as we had hoped for. Maybeth and I agreed that as long as there is life there is hope, but we felt that after death there is no hope if one is not adjusted to the laws and principles the Lord has set down. I promised my wife that I would do everything I could to help our children get right with God and be more concerned about the good things of life.
>
> In order to keep my promise, I analyzed the past and present, decided what improvements were needed and mapped out a plan to achieve those improvements. However, when I approached my children, they said I was too critical and felt I was trying to push them around. I was deeply puzzled as I watched them say they wanted to be good and do right, but uncomplainingly allowed people virtually devoid of Christian ideals push them around at will.

I recognized that I needed help, so I began to read the scriptures more, prayed more, and sought advice from people who had been in similar situations as mine. Maybeth had passed on, and I still felt that I needed more help, so I prayed — if it were not contrary to God's will — that He would allow Maybeth to help me from her vantage point.

As several days passed, my faith was beginning to waiver, but then I received my answer. My wife and a haggard-looking woman appeared to me in a dream. Maybeth dressed as she always had, and her back was hunched as it had been in life. She said,

"You do not just step into Heaven when you come up here. No one has a perfect record, and so everyone has to go through something like an atoning session, some longer than others, to clear up unforgiven wrongs. I went right at it and have almost completed mine. There were those who thought this woman should not have been admitted at all, because she had such a poor record, for though she has done some of her penance, she has a long way to go. Sometimes she gets discouraged and wants to give up, but we encourage her and she keeps trying. I have been assigned to her because I seem to get more work out of her than most anyone else. This is about the last of my atoning penalty. I have to get her back to work now."

I could find nothing in this dream that would help me with my immediate problem, but I did come to understand that paradise and heaven are not the same place. Paradise seems to be a place where we may put the finishing touches on our record, in preparation for entrance into a more perfect kingdom. This idea was very consoling to me, for I had never thought that we could be anything but absolutely perfect in order to make the next step toward the heavenly kingdom.

A few nights later I had another dream that starkly contrasted with the first. There stood Maybeth, alone in an open, meadow-like space with trees in the background, in all her glory, straight up without a hint of her hunchback, and no wrinkles, in an immaculate white evening dress, wearing a headdress that was between a crown and a turban. She stood there several minutes, neither moving nor speaking, while I stood several feet away and gazed at her. Her eyes indicated that she wanted to tell me something, but she could not talk. Then, in an instant she disappeared.

I still felt that this did not help me with my problem, but I realized, with gratitude, that Maybeth must have completed her atoning stint and was moving on into a more glorious realm.

Maybeth came to me once more, a few nights later. She remained inside a building that was in back of a wall or screen, but she talked to me for quite a while. In substance, she said that her message this time was an answer to my prayer, and was for our children, their families, and me. She hinted to me that we do not always get what we ask for when we pray because we do not always know what is the best way for us to obtain what we most desire.

Maybeth suggested that I remind our children and their families once more that no one can enter heaven without studying the scriptures and complying with their teachings. She wanted me to remind them that one of the surest ways to keep this command of God's is to attend church and associate at all times, if possible, with people who are concerned about obeying God's will. The ordinary person does not have enough willpower to constantly associate with people who are indifferent to the spiritual aspects of life and then hope to live in a way that is pleasing to God.

Lastly, I was to remind our children and families that no one can substitute for them in dealing with God. They will have to assume full responsibility for their actions and accept the consequences regardless of what they may be. Those who continue to be indifferent to God, who mock Him, or defy Him, will meet their doom at the grave. They will be stopped in their progress and thus separated from Him forever and ever. What a contrast this is with the fate of those who do His will and are privileged to share in His universe for eternity!

Then Maybeth admonished me that I should stop trying to pressure our children to do right. There is nothing that would please us more than to have them join us in a united family; however, we have taught them what is right and have urged them to do it. They are adults and must decide for themselves. My place now, she said, was to be there for them when they needed me.

Since this experience, I have tried to do all that Maybeth suggested.

Remembering that manifestations often teach principles in a symbolic way, and that each person's own perceptions will color his account of an occurrence, there is much that we find in this story to support the truths of the gospel. Immediately, we see the emphasis Maybeth and her husband placed on their family. It is interesting to consider that service may be the means by which we can make past wrongs right, as Maybeth's atoning stint was at least partially spent in helping another woman along. And finally, this series of dreams reminds us that the opportunity for eternal progression is a gift in this life whose continuation we must earn.

Questions and Answers

1. How are perfection and salvation achieved in the spirit world?

Joseph Smith taught that the intelligence man possesses is co-eternal with God himself. He compared man's existence to the endless nature of a ring, explaining that if man had a beginning he would also logically have an end.[3] Then he went on to say:

> The relationship we have with God places us in a situation to advance in knowledge. He has power to institute laws to instruct the weaker intelligences, that they may be exalted with himself, so that they might have one glory upon another, and all that knowledge, power, glory, and intelligence which is requisite in order to save them in the world of spirits...
>
> All things whatsoever God in His infinite wisdom has seen fit and proper to reveal to us, while we are dwelling in mortality, in regard to our mortal bodies, are revealed to...our spirits precisely as though we had no bodies at all; and those revelations which will save our spirits will save our bodies. God reveals them to us in view of no eternal dissolution of the body. Hence the responsibility, the awful responsibility, that rests upon us in relation to our dead; for all the spirits

---

[3]Smith, *Teachings of the Prophet Joseph Smith*, p. 301.

who have not obeyed the Gospel in the flesh must either obey it in the spirit or be damned...knowledge saves man; and in the world of spirits no man can be exalted but by knowledge. So long as a man will not give heed to the commandments, he must abide without salvation. If a man has knowledge, he can be saved; although if he has been guilty of great sins, he will be punished for them. But when he consents to obey the Gospel, whether here or in the world of spirits, he is saved.[4]

Clearly, then knowledge of true principles coupled with obedience is the saving power in this life and in the next.

Bruce C. Hafen indicated the need to make a distinction between two kinds of knowledge, only one of which is essential:

It is a fact of nature that salvation is a process, as well as a goal. Salvation involves growth, development, and change. That process implies that in mortality we must learn capacities and skills, not merely pick up information...The process of becoming Christlike is a matter of acquiring skills more than a matter of learning facts and figures. And there is something about the nature of developing those divine skills that makes it impossible even for God to teach us those things unless we participate in the process...knowing the Savior personally and emulating His example is the ultimate way of living the gospel, a way that transcends merely following specific com-

---

[4]Smith, *Teachings of the Prophet Joseph Smith*, pp. 352-353.

mandments and detailed doctrines...To learn by
example is to submit to authority... Hidden rules
can be assimilated only by a person who surren-
ders himself to that extent uncritically to the im-
itation of another.[5]

From this explanation, it is easy to see that perfection in or out of the body is achieved through
gaining a special kind of knowledge called skill development — acquiring the skill of emulating
Christ in every possible way. Doing this is a process
as well as a goal, continuing through this life and
the next. And the nature of our eternal work in becoming like Christ explains the reasons spirits perform the types of work they do.

2. *What kinds of things do disembodied spirits do*
    to progress?

We suggest that there are ten kinds of activities
or work that spirits do to progress in the spirit
world, and significantly, all but one of these activities, involve service:

1) Enduring the buffetings of Satan:

The scriptures plainly teach that some spirits
will have to endure the buffetings of Satan until
the day of redemption,[6] and Joseph Fielding Smith
explains that these spirits would seem to be subject
to Satan and he would have power to tempt them.
He suggests that perhaps the power of Satan to per-

---

[5]Bruce C. Hafen, "The Value of the Veil," *Ensign*, June 1977, pp. 10-13.

[6]See D&C 78:12, 82:21, 104:9, and 132:26.

suade them may be limited in the spirit world, but that at any rate, the buffeting would only last until the day of redemption.[7]

In his research, Dr. Moody was told repeatedly about a realm of bewildered spirits:

> One man recounted that the spirits he saw apparently "couldn't progress on the other side because their God is still living here." That is, they seemed bound to some particular object, person, or habit. Secondly, all have remarked that these beings appeared "dulled," that their consciences seemed somewhat limited in contrast with that of others. Thirdly, they say it appeared that these "dulled spirits" were to be there only until they solved whatever problem or difficulty was keeping them in that perplexed state.[8]

2) Gaining experience through work:

President Brigham Young taught:

> If we are striving with all the powers and faculties God has given us to improve upon our talents, to prepare ourselves to dwell in eternal life, and the grave receives our bodies while we are thus engaged, with what disposition will our spirits enter their next state? They will be still striving to do the things of God, only in a much

---

[7]Smith, *Answers to Gospel Questions*, V. 3, pp. 193-194.

[8]Moody, Raymond A. Jr., M.D. *Reflections on Life After Life*. St. Simons Island, Ga.: Mockingbird Books, 1977, p. 18.

greater degree — learning, increasing, growing in grace and in the knowledge of the truth.[9]

And Elder Rudger Clawson made a similar comment:

> What do the dead do?...in my opinion they are doing over there just exactly what we are doing here.[10]

3) Worship through music:

There is a great deal of evidence that music plays a significant role in the activities of the spirit world. One example is the heavenly choir that was heard by many at the dedication of the Manti Temple:

> A number of Saints in the body of the hall and some of the brethren in the west stand heard the most heavenly voices singing. It sounded to them as angelic, and appeared to be behind and above them, and many turned their heads in that direction wondering if there were not another choir in some other part of the building. There was no other choir, however.[11]

Another instance where spirits' singing has been heard by mortals was witnessed by David P. Kimball as recorded in this account:

---

[9]Brigham Young, *Journal of Discourses*, Vol. 7, p. 333.

[10]Rudger Clawson, in Conference Report, Apr. 1933, pp. 75-76.

[11]Lundwall, *Temples of the Most High*, p. 123.

. . . (I) heard the most beautiful singing I ever listened to in all my life. There were the words, repeated three times by a choir: "God bless Brother David Kimball." I at once distinguished among them the voice of my second wife, Julia Merrill, who in life was a good singer. This, of course, astonished me... After all this I gave way to doubt, thinking it might be only a dream, and to convince myself that I was awake, I got up and walked out doors into the open air. I returned and still the spirit of doubt was upon me. To test it further I asked my wife Julia to sing me a verse of one of her old songs. At that, the choir, which had continued singing, stopped and she sang the song through, every word being distinct and beautiful. The name of the song was, 'Does He Ever Think of Me?'...The singing commenced again, directly above me. I now wrapped myself in a pair of blankets and went out doors, determined to see the singers, but could see nothing, though I could hear the voices just the same. I returned to my couch and the singing, which was all communicative and instructive, continued until the day dawned.[12]

4) Growth through leadership:

Brigham Young taught that progression continues in the spirit world, where spirits move from one department to another just as we do in school when we change grades.[13] Wilford Woodruff

---

[12]Whitney, *Helpful Visions*, pp. 10-11.

[13]Brigham Young, *Journal of Discourses*, Vol. 3, p. 375 and Vol. 6, p. 349.

gained the same knowledge from a visitor beyond the veil:

> The thought came to me that Brother Joseph had left the work of watching over this church and kingdom to others, and that he had gone ahead, and that he had left this work to men who have lived and labored with us since he left us. This idea manifested itself to me, that such men advance in the spirit world.[14]

5) Preparing the way for ordinance work to be performed:

In Chapter 8 there were several examples of spirits helping with genealogy and ordinance work, and in Chapter 7 there was the unusual instance when James W. LeSueur visited the spirit world and discovered that he should seal his brother, Frank, to Jennie, a girl he had never known in this life. In spite of our certainty that spirits are involved, we do not know the exact details of how and what all they do. However, as Brother Ballard explained, the "time is coming when we will more fully understand this and the great bulk of the work will be done" (see page 189).

6) Record keeping and reporting:

We have shared several examples where record keeping has been emphasized as a duty in the spirit world, but instances of reporting are more rare.

---

[14]Wilford Woodruff, *Journal of Discourses*, Vol. 21, p. 318.

While on a mission, Thomas Shreeve had an unusual experience that clearly illustrates reporting:

> While I lay there...a personage clothed in a
> white robe entered the room. He appeared to be a
> young man and had a very pleasing counte-
> nance...[He] seated himself at the table and
> opened a book. He said: "Are you ready to report
> the Sydney Branch?" "Yes, sir," I responded.
> "Then proceed." I gave him an account of all our
> doings in Sydney, beginning with our first effort
> of reorganizing and closing with my last act pre-
> vious to sailing — for all these things seemed
> plain to my mind.
>
> The recital seemed to occupy me several min-
> utes and I continued to speak freely. He wrote in
> the books rapidly, and never once interrupted
> me. I felt that he was taking every work I uttered.
> When I stopped, he asked, "Have you anything
> more to say?" "No, sir," I answered. Then he
> turned the leaves back, and seemed to read from
> the beginning, He said: "Very well. Now where
> are you going?" "To New Zealand." He recorded
> my answer in the book and signed his name — I
> could not see the words of his name, but I felt that
> he was writing his own signature.
>
> He closed the book and walked around to the
> right side of the bed, shook hands with me, and
> said: "Good-by; I will be there before you."[15]

---

[15]Thomas A. Shreeve, "Finding Comfort," *Helpful Visions*. Salt Lake City,
Ut.: Juvenile Instructor Office, 1887, pp. 59-60.

7) Preparing for prophetic events such as the Second Coming:

There is much information on this topic, but this statement by President Brigham Young suggests that some planning and decision-making must be done before important events:

> They are preaching, preaching all the time and preparing the way for us to hasten our work in building temples here and elsewhere, and to go back to Jackson County and build the great temple of the Lord. They are hurrying to get ready by the time that we are ready, and we are all hurrying to get ready by the time our Elder Brother is ready. . . .[16]

8) Ministering servants to other spirits or guardian angels to mortals:

In Chapter 3 we dealt at some length with guardian angels. It appears that this is a major activity of some spirits, but there is another type of activity related to it that we ought to consider — that of ministering servants. The Prophet Joseph Smith taught:

> The spirits of just men are made ministering servants to those who are sealed unto life eternal, and it is through them that the sealing power comes down. . . .[17]

---

[16]Brigham Young, *Journal of Discourses*, Vol. 3, pp. 370-372.

[17]Joseph Smith, *History of the Church*, Vol. 6, p. 51.

9) *Missionary Work:*

After reading Chapter 7, it should be quite clear that missionary activity is the greatest work in the spirit world.

10) *Genealogical and Temple Work:*

Again, all of Chapter 8 was devoted to this important work.

This list of spirits' activities cannot hope to be all-inclusive, but it gives us a general feel for their work and for what things are of more than earthly importance.

Epilogue

During the night of January 20th, 1920, while staying alone in a room of the W.J. Brawson home in Carey, Idaho, Heber Q. Hale had a spiritual manifestation of immense proportions. In fact, it touched on nearly every aspect we have considered in this book, and therefore we have chosen it as a final witness to the nature of the spirit world.

The experience took place sometime between twelve and seven-thirty, and Brother Hale noted that during that time he neither turned over in bed nor was disturbed by any sounds, something very unusual for him. He also did not know whether this was a dream, an apparition, a vision, or a pilgrimage of his spirit into the next world, but he was without doubt that he actually saw these things and that they were as real to him as any other experiences of his life. Brother Hale explained:

> I passed but a short distance from my body through a film in the world of spirits, this was my first experience after going to sleep. I seemed to realize I had passed through the change called death and so referred to it in my conversation with the immortal beings with whom I became immediately in contact. I readily observed their displeasure of the use of the word 'death' and the fear which we attach to it, they use there another word in referring to the transition from mortality, which word I do not now recall. I can only

approach its meaning as the impression was left upon my mind, by calling it the New Birth.

My first visual impression was the nearness of the world of spirits to the world of mortality. The vastness of this heavenly sphere was bewildering to the eyes of a spirit. Many enjoyed unrestricted freedom as to both vision and action. The vegetation or landscape was beautiful beyond description, not all green, but gold and various shades of pink, orange, and lavender as the rainbow. A sweet calmness pervaded everything. The people I met there I did not think of as spirits, but as men and women, self-thinking, self-acting individuals going about important business in a most orderly manner. There was perfect order and everyone had something to do and seemed to be about their business.

That the inhabitants of the spirit world are classified according to their lives of purity and their obedience to the Father's will was subsequently made apparent. Particularly was it observed that the wicked and unrepentant are confined to a certain district by themselves, the confines of which are so definitely determined and impassible as the line marking the vision of the physical and spiritual world, a mere film but impassible until the person himself has changed. The world of spirits is the temporary abode of all spirits, pending the resurrection from the dead and the judgment.

There was much activity within the different spheres and appointed ministers of salvation were soon coming from the higher to the lower in pursuit of their missionary appointments. I had a very pronounced desire to meet certain of my kinfolk and friends, but I was at once im-

pressed with the fact that I had entered a tremen-
dously great and extensive world, even greater
than our earth and more numerously inhabited.
I could be in only one place at a time, could look
in only one direction at a time and accordingly it
would require many, many years to search out
and converse with all those I had known and
those whom I desired to meet, unless they were
especially summoned to receive me.

All worthy men and women were appointed
to special and regular work, under a well-orga-
nized plan of action, directed principally toward
preaching the gospel to the unconverted, teaching
those who seek knowledge and establishing family relationships and gathering genealogies for
the use and benefit of mortal survivors of their
respective families, that the work of baptism and
sealing ordinances may be vicariously performed
for the departed in the temples of God on earth.

The authorized representatives of families in
the world of spirits have access to our temple
records and are kept fully advised to the work
therein, but the vicarious work done here does
not become automatically effective there. The recipients must first repent and accept baptism and
confirmation. Then certain consummating ordinances are performed effectualizing these same
principles in the lives of those regenerated beings. So the great work is going on — they are
doing a work there which we cannot do here, and
we are doing a work here which they cannot do,
both necessary, each the compliment of the other.
Thus, it is bringing about the salvation of all
God's children, who will be saved.

I was surprised to find there no babes in arms. I met the infant son of Arson W. Rawlins, my first counselor, and immediately recognized him as the baby who died a few years ago. Yet he seemed to have the intelligence and in certain respects the appearance of an adult and was engaged in matters pertaining to his family and its genealogy. My mind was quite contented on the point that mothers will again receive into their arms their children who die in infancy and will be fully satisfied, but the fact remains that entrance into the world of spirits is not an inhibition of growth but a great opportunity for development. Babies are adult spirits in infant bodies.

I presently beheld a mighty multitude of men — the largest I had ever seen gathered in one place, whom I immediately recognized as soldiers; the millions who had been slaughtered and rushed so savagely into the world of spirits during the World War.[1]

Among them moved calmly and majestically a great general in supreme command. As I drew near, I received the kindly smile and generous welcome of the great living General, Richard W. Young. Then came the positive conviction to my soul that of all men living or dead, there is not one who is so perfectly fitted for the great mission into which he had been called. He commands immediately the attention and respect of all soldiers. He is at once a great general and a High Priest of God, no earthly field of labor to which he could have been assigned can compare with it in importance and extent.

---

[1]Referring to World War I.

I passed from this scene to return later, when I found General Young had this vast army of men completely organized with officers over successive divisions and all were seated and he was preaching the Gospel in great earnestness to them.

As I passed on, I met my beloved mother. She greeted me most affectionately and expressed surprise at seeing me there and reminded me that I had not completed my allotted mission on earth. She seemed to be going somewhere and was in a hurry and accordingly took leave, saying she would see me again.

I moved forward covering an appreciable distance and consuming considerable time viewing the wonderful landscapes, parks, trees, and flowers, and meeting people, some of whom I knew but many thousands whom I did not recognize. I presently approached a small group of men standing in a path lined with spacious stretches of flowers, grasses and shrubbery, all of a golden hue, marking the approach to a beautiful building. The group was engaged in earnest conversation. One of their number parted from the rest and came walking down the path. I at once recognized my esteemed President Joseph F. Smith. He embraced me as a father would a son and after a few words of greeting quickly remarked, "You have not come to stay," which remark I understood more as a declaration than an interrogation.

For the first time I became fully aware of my incomplete mission on earth and as much as I would have liked to remain, I at once asked President Smith if I might return. "You have expressed a righteous desire," he replied, "and I shall take the matter up with the authorities and let you know later." He then turned and led me toward the little group of men from whom he was just separated. I immediately recognized Brigham Young and the Prophet Joseph Smith, and was surprised to find the former of shorter and heavier build than I expected to find him. All three of these men were in possession of a calm and holy majesty, which was at once kind and kingly. President Smith, introduced me to the others, who greeted me warmly. We then returned our steps and President Smith took his leave, saying he would see me again.

From a certain point of vantage, I was permitted to view this earth and what was going on here. There were no limitations to my vision and I was astonished at this. I saw my wife and children at home; I saw President Heber J. Grant at the head of the Church and Kingdom of God, and felt the divine power that radiated from God giving it light and truth, guiding its destiny. I beheld this nation founded as it is upon correct principles and designed to endure and beset by evil and sinister forces that seek to lead men astray and thwart the purpose of God. I saw towns and cities, the sin and wickedness of men and women. I saw vessels sailing upon the ocean and scanned the battle-scarred fields of France and Belgium. In a word I saw the whole world as if it were a panorama passing before my eyes.

Then there came to me the unmistakable impression that this earth and persons upon it are open to the visions of the spirits only when special permission is given or when they are assigned to special service here. This is particularly true of the righteous who are busily engaged in the service of the Lord and cannot be engaged in two fields of activity at the same time.

The wicked and unrepentant spirits having still their free agency and applying themselves to no useful or wholesome undertaking, seek pleasure about their old haunts to this extent they are still tools of Satan. It is idle, mischievous, and deceptive spirits who appear as miserable counterfeits at spiritualistic scenes, table dancing, and other such things. The noble and great men do not respond at the call of the mediums and every curious group of meddlesome inquiries. They would not do it in mortality, certainly they would not do it in their increased state of knowledge in the world of immortality. These wicked and unrepentant spirits are allies of Satan and his hosts operating through willing mediums in the flesh. These three forces constitute an unholy trinity upon the earth and are responsible for all the wickedness among men and nations.

I moved forward, feasting my eyes upon the beauty, everything about me was glorying in the indescribable peace and happiness which abounded in everybody and through everything. The farther I went the more glorious things appeared.

While standing at a certain vantage point I beheld a short distance away a wonderfully beautiful temple, capped with golden domes, from which emerged a small group of men dressed in robes, who paused for a brief conversation. These were the first I had seen thus clad. The millions I had previously seen were dressed of course, but dressed variously, the soldiers for instance were in uniform. In this little group of holy men my eyes rested upon one more splendid and holy than all the rest. While thus I gazed, President Smith parted from the others and came to my side.

"Do you know Him?" he inquired. I quickly answered, "Yes, I know Him." My eyes beheld my Lord and Savior. "It is true," said President Joseph F. Smith. O how my soul filled with rapture and unspeakable joy. President Smith informed me that I had been given permission to return and complete my mission upon the earth which the Lord had appointed me to fill, and then with his hand upon my shoulder uttered those memorable and significant words:

"Brother Heber, you have a great work to do, go forward with all your heart and you shall be blessed in your ministry. From this time on never doubt that God lives, that Jesus Christ is His Son, the Redeemer of the world, that the Holy Ghost is a God of spirit and the messenger of the Father and the Son. Never doubt the resurrection of the dead and the immortality of the soul. The mission of Latter-day Saints is to all the world, both living and dead. The great work in the Holy Temple for the salvation of the dead is only begun. Know that Joseph Smith was a Son of God, to usher in the Gospel dispensation of the fullness of times which is the last unto mortals on this earth. His successors have all been called and approved by God. President Heber J. Grant is at this time the recognized and ordained head of the Church of Jesus Christ upon the earth. Give him your confidence and support. Much you have seen and heard here you will not be permitted to repeat when you return." Thus saying, he bade me good-by and God bless you.

Quite a distance through various scenes and passing innumerable people, I traveled before I reached this sphere which I had first entered on my way. I was greeted by many friends and relatives, certain of whom sent words of greetings and counsel to dear ones here, my brother being one of them.

One other I will mention, I met Brother John Adamson, his wife, son James, and daughter Isabelle, all of whom were killed by the hand of a foul assassin at Carey, Idaho on the evening of October 29, 1915. They seemed to define that I was on my way back to mortality and immediately said: (Brother Adamson speaking) "Tell the children we are very happy and that they should not mourn our departure nor worry their minds over the manner by which we were taken. There is a purpose in it and we have work here to do which requires our collective efforts and which we could not do individually."

I was made to know that the work referred to was that of genealogy in which they were working in England and Scotland. One of the greatest and most sacred things of heaven is family relationships, the establishment of a complete chain without a broken link. The unholy and bad will be dropped out and other new links put in, or two adjoining links welded together. Men and women throughout the world are moved upon by their dead ancestors to gather genealogy. These are the links of the chains, and the ordinances of baptism, endowments and sealings performed in the Temple of God by the living for the dead are the welding of the links.

Ordinances are performed in the spirit world effectualizing in the individual recipients, the saving principles of the gospel vicariously performed here. As I was approaching the place where I had entered, my attention was attracted to a small group of women preparing what appeared to be wearing apparel. Observing my inquiring countenance, one of the women remarked, "We are preparing to receive Brother Philip Worthington soon." (I was advised by telegram that he died January 22, and I returned to Boise to preach the funeral sermon January 23.)

As I gasped his name in repetition, I was admonished, "If you knew the joy and glorious mission that awaits him you would not ask to have him longer detained on earth."

Then flooding through my consciousness came this truth, that the will of the Lord can be done on earth as it is in heaven, only when we resign completely to His will and let His will be done in innocence and peace. Many have passed a life of suffering and misery and are full of debauchery and crime and have lived to their own peril. Men and women and children are often called to missions of great importance on the other side and some respond gladly while others refuse to go and their loved ones will not give them up. Also many die because they have not faith to be healed. Others yet live long and pass out of this world of mortality without any special manifestations or actions of the divine will.

When a man is stricken ill, the prime importance is not whether he lives or dies, so long as the Father's will be done. Surely we can trust him with God. Herein lies the special duty and privilege of administration by the Holy Priesthood — namely, it is given the elders of the

Church, to divine the will of the Father concerning the one upon whose head their hands are laid. If for any reason they are unable to presage the Father's will, then they shall continue to pray in faith for the afflicted, humbly conceding supremacy to the will of God, that His will be done on earth as it is in heaven.

Birth into the world of spirits is a glorious privilege and blessing, the greatest spirits in the family of the Father have not usually been permitted to tarry longer in the flesh than to perform a certain mission. They are then called to the world of spirit where the field is greater and workers fewer. This earthly career, then, may be long or short.

At that time I left the world of spirits, and immediately my body was quickened, and I arose to ponder over and now declare to the world, that irrespective of what others may say or think, I do know of my own positive knowledge and from my own personal experiences that Jesus Christ is *His* son and Savior of the world.

I also bear witness to these things: That the spirit of man does not die, but survives this change called death and goes to the world of spirit. That the world of spirit is upon or near this world, that man's individuality is not lost by death nor his progress inhibited. The spirits will literally take up their bodies again in the resurrection. That the principles of salvation are now being taught to the spirits and the great work of saving the Father's family among the living and dead is in progress, and but comparatively few will be lost. That the Gospel of Jesus Christ has again been established upon the earth with all the keys, powers, authority and blessings

through the instrumentality of the Prophet
Joseph Smith. That this is not only the power
which will save and exalt everyone obedient, but
will ultimately save the world, that the burden of
our mission is to save souls unto God. And that
the work for the dead is no less important than
the work for the living.[2]

What a glorious manifestation and an
exhilarating testimony Brother Hale bears witness
of! Yet, as we end this collection of experiences and
testimonies, we feel it is correct to reconsider the
premise upon which we began: that the study of
knowledge beyond the veil should work to support
the first principles of the gospel and strengthen our
belief in them.

Based on what we have read, we should have a
new understanding of this life as well as the life to
come. We should look with new eyes on the vital
nature of our family relationships. How could we
doubt our Savior's love or think that our reward
could be less than any sacrifice or service we are
called upon to perform? And above all, how could
we retain any fear of death itself if we exercise the
eternal perspective we have glimpsed?

This increased understanding should leave us
with a new and potent gratitude for the veil our
Heavenly Father has mercifully placed between this
earthly existence and our first and third estates. The
veil is not there to forever bar us from God's

[2]Heber Q. Hale, "A Heavenly Manifestation by Heber Q. Hale, President of
the Boise Stake of the Church of Jesus Christ of Latter-day Saints," Jan. 20,
1920 (unpublished manuscript).

knowledge and presence but to tutor us so that we may become ready to be there. Because of it, mortality is able to teach us about obedience, show us the value of working for our reward, give us the chance to develop faith, help us understand the real meaning of patience, and allow us to truly exercise our free agency. Our attitude toward the veil should be filled with anticipation for our turn to pass beyond, and yet contain a healthy desire to live this life at our best, understanding that our time is not yet. Above all, we see that the veil and the glories beyond bear witness to the loving care of our Father in Heaven.

Bibliography

Scriptural Sources:

The Book of Mormon. Joseph Smith Jr. (trans.) Salt Lake City: The Church of Jesus Christ of Latter-day Saints, 1981.

The Doctrine and Covenants of The Church of Jesus Christ of Latter-day Saints. Salt Lake City: The Church of Jesus Christ of Latter-day Saints, 1981.

The Pearl of Great Price. Salt Lake City: The Church of Jesus Christ of Latter-day Saints, 1981.

The Holy Bible. The New King James Translation; Salt Lake City: The Church of Jesus Christ of Latter-day Saints, 1981.

Books:

Allred, Gordon T. *If A Man Die*. Salt Lake City: Bookcraft Inc., 1964.

Ballard, Melvin J. *Three Degrees of Glory — A Discourse*. Salt Lake City: Magazine Printing Co., 1955.

Burton, Alma P. & Clea M. (comp.) *For They Shall Be Comforted*. Salt Lake City: Deseret Book Co., 1964.

Callis, Charles A. *Fundamentals of Religion*. Salt Lake City: Deseret Book Co., 1945.

Clark, James R. *Messages of the First Presidency*. Salt Lake City: Bookcraft Inc., 1965.

Crowther, Duane S. *Life Everlasting*. Salt Lake City: Bookcraft Inc., 1967.

Evans, Richard L. *Richard Evans' Quote Book*. Salt Lake City: Publishers Press, 1971.

Hackworth, Dorothy South. *The Master's Touch*. Salt Lake City: Bookcraft Inc., 1961.

Hinckley, Bryant S. *The Faith of Our Pioneer Fathers*. Salt Lake City: Deseret Book Co., 1959.

Journal of Discourses. 26 vols. Los Angeles: General Printing and Lithograph Co., 1961. (Photo lithographic reprint of exact original edition published in 1882).

Kenyon. "Briant S. Stevens," *Helpful Visions*. Salt Lake City: Juvenile Instructor Office, 1887.

Kimball, Abraham A. "Finding A Father," *Gems For the Young Folks*. Salt Lake City: Juvenile Instructor Office, 1881.

Kimball, Edward L. *The Teachings of Spencer W. Kimball*. Salt Lake City: Bookcraft Inc., 1982.

Kimball, Spencer W. *The Miracle of Forgiveness*. Salt Lake City: Bookcraft, Inc. 1969.

Kimball, Spencer W. *Tragedy or Destiny?* Salt Lake City: Deseret Book Co., 1977.

Kuebler-Ross, Elizabeth, *On Death and Dying*, New York: MacMillan, 1969.

Lundwall, N.B. *Temples of the Most High*, 10th ed. Salt Lake City, Bookcraft Inc., 1941.

McConkie, Bruce R. (comp.) *Doctrines of Salvation — Sermons and Writings of Joseph Fielding Smith*, 3 vols. Salt Lake City: Bookcraft Inc., 1954-1956.

McConkie, Bruce R. *Mormon Doctrine*, 2nd ed. Salt Lake City: Bookcraft Inc., 1966.

Moody, Raymond A. Jr., M.D. *Life After Life*. St. Simons Island, Georgia: Mockingbird Books, 1975.

Moody, Raymond A. Jr., M.D. *Reflections on Life After Life*. St. Simons Island, Georgia: Mockingbird Books, 1977.

Nibley, Preston (comp.) *Sharing the Gospel with Others: Excerpts from Sermons of President Smith*. Salt Lake City: Deseret Book Co., 1948.

Packer, Boyd K. *That All May Be Edified*. Salt Lake City: Bookcraft Inc., 1982.

Packer, Boyd K. *The Holy Temple*. Salt Lake City: Bookcraft Inc., 1980.

Pratt, Parley P. *Autobiography of Parley P. Pratt*, 6th ed., Salt Lake City: Deseret Book Co., 1966.

Pratt, Parley P. *Key to Science and Theology*, 10th ed., Salt Lake City: Deseret Book Co., 1966.

Rickenbacker, Edward Vernon. *The Autobiograpy of Eddie Rickenbacker*. Englewood Cliffs, N.J.: Prentice-Hall, 1967.

Ritchie, George G., M.D. *Return From Tomorrow*. Old Tappan, New Jersey: Fleming H. Revell Co., 1978.

Shreeve, Thomas A. "Finding Comfort," *Helpful Visions*. Salt Lake City: Juvenile Instructor Office, 1887.

Smith, Joseph. *History of The Church of Jesus Christ of Latter-day Saints*, 7 vols, 2nd ed., Salt Lake City: Deseret Book Co., 1959.

Smith, Joseph F. *Gospel Doctrine*. Salt Lake City: Deseret Book Co., 1919.

Smith, Joseph Fielding. *Answers to Gospel Questions*, 3 vols. Salt Lake City: Deseret Book Co., 1959.

Smith, Joseph Fielding (comp.). *Teachings of the Prophet Joseph Smith*. Salt Lake City: The Deseret News Press, 1938.

Tagg, Melvin Salway. *The Life of Edward James Wood*. Provo,
    Utah: Master's Thesis, College of Religious Instruction,
    BYU (published by author), 1959.

Whitney, Orson F. "A Terrible Ordeal," *Helpful Visions*. Salt
    Lake City: Juvenile Instructor Office, 1887.

Wixom, Hartt and Judene. *Trial by Terror*. Horizon Publishers:
    Bountiful, Utah, 1987.

Woodruff, Wilford. *Leaves From My Journal*, 4th ed., Salt Lake
    City: The Deseret News, 1949.

Young, Lorenzo Dow. "Lorenzo Dow Young's Narrative,"
    Fragments of Experience. Salt Lake City: Juvenile Instructor
    Office, 1882.

Periodicals:

Campbell, Avril Marie. "When Julie Died," *Ensign*. August
    1977., pp. 56-57.

Clawson, Rudger. *Conference Report*. Apr. 1933, pp. 75-76.

Fisher, Terry Lynn. "Please Do My Work," *Ensign*. August,
    1983, pp. 54-55.

Hafen, Bruce C. "The Value of the Veil," *Ensign*. June 1977, pp.
    10-13.

Johnson, Peter E. "A Testimony," *The Relief Society Magazine*,
    vol. VII, no. 8. August, 1920.

Kimball, Spencer W. "The Things of Eternity — Stand We in
    Jeopardy?" *Ensign*. January, 1977, pp. 4-6.

Lyman, Francis M. *Conference Report*, October 1909, p. 18.

"Manifestation About Building Temples," *Deseret Evening
    News*. May 18, 1918.

Maxwell, Neal A. "Patience" *Ensign*. October, 1980, p. 31.

McConkie, Bruce R. *Conference Report*, April, 1985, pp. 9-12.

McConkie, Bruce R. *Conference Report*, October, 1976, pp. 157-159.

Monson, Thomas S. *Ensign*, April 1982, p. 9.

Peterson, John "Was Dead and Came to Life Again," *Millenial Star*, vol. 68, 1916, p. 699.

Sill, Sterling W. *Conference Report*, October, 1976.

Smith, Hyrum G. *Conference Report*, April, 1917, pp. 70-71.

Smith, Joseph F. *Conference Report*, October, 1899, pp. 20-21.

Smith, Joseph F. *Young Women's Journal*, Mar. 1912, p. 130.

Snow, LeRoi C. "Raised From the Dead," *Improvement Era*. vol. 32 no. 12. October, 1929.

Spicer, J. Pat. "In An Old Country Church," *Ensign*. April, 1983, p. 29.

Utah Genealogical and Historical Magazine, Vol. 23:148-149.

Unpublished Manuscripts:

Benson, Ezra Taft. Address given at Regional Representatives' Seminar, Apr. 3, 1981.

Hale, Heber Q. "A Heavenly Manifestation by Heber Q. Hale, President of the Boise Stake of The Church of Jesus Christ of Latter-day Saints," January 20, 1920. (mimeographed)

LeSueur, James A. "A Peep in the Spirit World," (mimeographed)

Packer, Boyd K. Address given at genealogical seminar. August 6, 1970.

Zollinger, Henry. "My Experience in the Spirit World." (manuscript)

Index

Adam: 126

Abraham: prologue vii

Accidental death: 24-26

Addictions: 75-76, 100, 199

Age: 56-58, 209

Alma: 96-97

Angel: 47, 52, 54-55, 79, 97, 119

Animals: 104-105, 119

Annie: 116-117

Appearances: 37, 44, 80-81, see also "Spirits"

Architecture: 107-109, 111, 113-115, 116-117, 212, see also "Buildings"

Atonement: 92

Audrey: 174-178

Aura: mortals', 94-95, 100, 112-113; spirits', see "Bright light," and "Being of light"

Authority: 124-129, 138-139, 159, 161-162

Ballard, Melvin J.: 76, 155 footnote #4, 188-189, 202

Baptism: 151, 182, 187, 208, 214; see also "Ordinances"

Being of light: 47-49

Benson, Ezra Taft: 156, 181

Birds: 42

Birth: 11-12

Blatchford, Robert: 10

Body: separation from spirit, 9, 12-13, 76, 77-79, 136-137, 138-141, 207

Bright light: 5, 37, 44, 47-49, 51, 90, 93, 107, 176

Brooks, David Lynn: 162

Brown, Hugh B.: 13-14

Buildings: 105, 107-109, 111-112, 113-117, 120-122, 150-151, 193, 212

Callis, Charles A.: 34-35

Campbell, Avril Marie: 51

Carma: 106-110, 120

Carr, Brother: 172-174

Cdekirk, Nellie: 154

Children: 24-29, 56-58, 111, 209

Cicero: 23

Clark, James R.: 101

Clawson, Rudger: 200

Clothing: of spirits, 44, 54-56, 105, 109, 130, 150, 209, 212, 215

Comfort: 39-45
Communication: prologue
    iii, 18-19, 33-34, 37, 44, 49-
    52, 76, 100, 105-106, 193,
    201
Computers: 108, 114, 121
Corianton: 96-97
Creation: 81, 112 footnote
    #2, 118-120
Cutler, Alphaeus: 131-132,
    140

Darkness: 47, 49 footnote
    #13, 97, 107, 113
Death: common elements
    of, 16-18; meaning of, 9-
    11, 206-207; see also
    "Fear" and "Untimely"
Die in the Lord: 21-22
Dimensions: 90, 100
Discerning of spirits: 74
Dreams: 49-50
Duality: 112 footnote #2,
    118-120

Early death a blessing: 24-25
Earth: 106-107, 130-131, 135,
    211
Education: see
    "Progression" and
    "Schooling"
Edwards, Tyron: 9

Effects of experiences:
    prologue vi-vii, ix-x, 3,
    6, 38, 142, 155-156
Elijah: 171
Environment: see "Spirit
    world"
Evans, Charles D.: 153-154

Family: 38, 41, 66-69, 110,
    111, 113, 116, 122-123,
    156-157, 165-181, 182-189,
    194-195, 208, 214
Fear: 19-20, 39, 40-41, 92, 217
Fighting: 100-153
First principles of the
    gospel: 151-152, 217
Flowers: 42, 105-106, 107,
    108, 111, 117, 119, 210
Forgiveness: 90; see also
    "Repentance"
Free agency: 25-26, 98, 212,
    218
Friends: 46, 122-123

Gardens: 111-112
Gate: 105
Genealogy: 141, 148-149,
    151, 162, 165-181, 182-189,
    202, 205, 214
Ghosts: 71
Government: 124-125
Grant, Heber J.: 26-29, 138,
    211

Grant, Jedediah M.:110-113,
    118-119, 120
Guardian angel: 65, 70-74,
    93, 100, 150, 187-188, 204
Guide: 48, 72, 73, 167

Habits: 75-76, 190
Hafen, Bruce C.: 197
Hale, Heber Q.: 56-57, 206-
    217
Hamblin, Jacob: 130-131
Hawthorn, Nathaniel: 13
Healing: see "Priesthood
    blessings"
Hell: see "Spirit prison"
Henry: 127
Hinckley, Alonzo: 55-56

Inclinations : 75-76, 190
Individuality: 75-76, 80-81
Ineffability: 18
Intelligence: 75, 78, 91, 196-
    197
Isaiah: 47, 184

Jensen, Ella: 14-15, 55, 56-57,
    119, 140, 163
Johnson, Loaz: 191-195
Johnson, Peter E.: 15, 165-
    171
Jose: 104-106
Judgment: 87-95, 96-97, 191

Kimball, Abraham A.: 131

Kimball David P.: 72, 120-
    121, 141, 200-201
Kimball, Heber C.: 53, 110-
    113, 136
Kimball, Spencer W.: 25,
    102, 137, 156-157, 183
Knowledge: 78, 92, 142, 163,
    196-198
Kuebler-Ross, Elizabeth: 18-
    19

Lang, John M.: 186-187
Lazarus: raised from the
    dead, prologue vii;
    beggar, 140
Leadership: 201-202
Learning: see
    "Progression," and
    "Schools," and also
    "Knowledge"
Leon: 7-8
LeSueur, Frank: see
    "LeSueur, James"
LeSueur, James W.: 147-
    156, 162, 202
Light: see "Aura," "Bright
    light," and also "Being
    of light"
Ligia: 43-45, 55
Link: 214
Lloyd: 59-62
Love: prologue iii, 34, 37,
    142, 178, 217, 218
Lund, Anthon H.: 185-186

Lyman, Francis M.: 23
Lynn: 40-41

Mansion: 116-117
Manti Temple: 185, 200
Margaret: 132-133
Marie: 33-34
Marriage: see "Sealings"
    and also "Ordinances"
Matter: 82
Maybeth: 191-195
Maughan, Peter: 127
Maxwell, Neal A. : 124
McConkie, Bruce R.: 11, 21,
    75, 100-101, 102-103, 158
McKay, David O.: 20
Mike: 39
Milman: 24
Ministering angel: 204
Missionary work: 145-157,
    158-165, 205, 207
Monson, Walter P.: 15-16,
    140
Moody, Raymond R., M.D.:
    16-18, 47-48, 50-51, 97,
    103, 119, 141, 142
    footnote #13, 199
Mourning: 22-24, 41
Movement : 77, 153
Music: 14, 114, 200-201; see
    also "Singing"

Neville, Eliza Dean: 54, 188
Noise: 17

Nola: 113-116, 120

Obedience: 163-164, 196-197,
    207, 218
Order: 110-111, 207; of Zion,
    120; see also
    "Organization"
Ordinances: 151, 156, 161,
    182-188, 202, 214
Organization: 110-111, 113,
    119, 121, 156, 159, 161-
    162, 208, 210

Packer, Boyd K.: 9, 178-179
Pain: lack of/relief from,
    prologue ii-iii, 5, 13-16,
    36, 42, 77, 160; in
    returning, prologue v, 6,
    15, 37, 43, 94, 133, 174; see
    also "Spirit prison"
Paradise: 97, 99-100, 116,
    122-123, 173, 192; see also
    "Spirit world"
Pat: 179-180
Paul: 182
Peace: prologue iii, 3, 7, 17-
    18, 97, 139, 173
Penance: 192
Perceptions: prologue ix,
    48, 55, 78, 79, 94
Perfection: 181, 198
Permission: 127, 138
Personality: 75, 76, 80-81;
    see also "Spirit"

Peterson, John: 73, 136, 162-163
Power: 159, 196-197, 217
Pratt, Orson: 78
Pratt, Parley P.: 48 footnote #13, 49-50, 71, 99 footnote #5, 160-161
Prayer: 44, 148-149, 150, 187, 192-193
Preliminary judgment: 87-96, 96-97
Pre-mortal spirits: 58
Priesthood: 125-126, 160, 161-162; blessings to restore health or life, prologue vi, 6-7, 12, 37, 129-130, 131, 134-135, 138-140; blessings to release, 34, 172-173, 215-216

Progression: 99, 145, 156, 174, 190, 195, 198-205
Protector: see "Guardian angels"
Punishment: 99-100
Puppy: 104-106
Purgatory: 191

Randy: 5-7
Rationale for study of spirit world: prologue viii
Raymond, Rossiter Worthington: 9

Realm of bewildered spirits: 99-100, 199
Recognizability: 80-81
Record keeping: 202-203
Recording angel: 187-188, 202-203
Redemption of the dead: 99; see also "Genealogy"
Relatives: 65, 115, 122-123, 167, 181, 183, 214; see also "Family"
Repentance: 76, 89-90, 159, 183
Reporting: 167, 187-188, 202-203
Resurrected beings: 47, 79-80, 83, 168
Resurrection: 97-98, 138-139, 168, 182
Return: 113, 129-135; choice, prologue v, 93-94, 137-138, 168-170, 176
Revelation: types of, prologue x
Review: 87-95, 96-97
Richard: 2-4
Richter, Jean Paul: 41
Rickenbacker, Eddie: 135
Ritchie, George C., M.D.: 48-49, 76, 100, 103, 121
Rodney: 42-43
Rose: 117
Roskelley, Bishop: 127

Sacredness of experiences:
    prologue ix, 4, 6, 38
Saving power: 196-197
Schools: 153, 163, 173; see
    also "Progression"
Scientific evidence: 16-19
Sealing: 155 footnote #4,
    156, 173, 204, 214
Senses: 78
Service: 165-189, 198-205,
    217
Shreeve, Thomas: 203
Singing: 14, 200-201
Smith, Alvin: 35 footnote
    #2
Smith, George Albert: 87-89
Smith, Hyrum: 168
Smith, Hyrum G.: 26
Snow, Eliza R.: 163
Snow, Erastus: 81
Snow, Lorenzo: 140, 164
Smith, Joseph: prologue
    viii, 24-25, 45, 46, 47, 51-
    52, 73, 79, 82, 82-83, 97,
    99-100, 119 footnote #7,
    123, 125, 126, 131, 158,
    163, 168, 181, 182, 184,
    196-197, 202, 204, 211, 217
Smith, Joseph F.: 23-24, 52-
    53, 56, 70-71, 74, 80, 122-
    123, 125, 137-138, 152
    footnote #2, 157, 159,
    161, 172, 210-211

Smith Joseph Fielding: 98,
    198-199
Socrates: 19
Southgate, Sister: 172-174
Spirits: knowledge of
    mortals, 45, 52-54, 56-59,
    70-74; evil, 49 footnote
    #13, 75, 207, 212; visiting
    privileges, 70-74, 127;
    visual abilities, prologue
    iv, 3, 5-6, 78, 88, 169-170,
    207, 211
Spirits of just men made
    perfect: 47, 79, 204
Spirit world: description of,
    87-88, 104-117, 207, 210;
    location of, 33, 99; Lord's
    presence, 83, 213;
    vegetation, 87-88, 105-
    106, 108, 111-112, 207, 210
Spirit prison: 99-100, 119,
    122, 207
Spiritual gifts: 74-75
St. George Temple: 173,
    186-187
Stael, Madame de: 41
Stevens, Briant: 77
Stewardship: 126-129
Study: see "Schools" and
    also "Progression"
Suicide: 100-103
Sunday School/Primary:
    see "Schools"

Supernatural rescues: 59-
61, 62-64, 66-69

Tangibility: 79-80, 82
Taylor, John: 125, 184
Teaching: 151, 162-163
Telepathic: prologue iii, 44,
49-52
Temple work: 165-189, 205
Temples: spirit world, 107-
108, 112; earthly, 120, 151,
170, 173, 180, 183, 184,
205; see also "Manti
Temple" and "St.
George Temple"
Temptation: 159-160
Theocracy: 124-125
Thought patterns: 49
Time: 123-124
Tithing: 54
Tunnel: 7-8, 17-18

Untimely death: 24-26, 145

Veil: prologue vi-ix, 33, 98,
217-218
Verbal communication: 51-
52, see also
"Communication"
Vicarious ordinances: 151,
155, 161, 182-183, 187-188,
208
Vision of the Redemption
of the Dead: 74

Whitney, Orson F.: 65, 70
Wilcox, Ella Wheeler: 47
Wilder, Thornton: 22
Woodruff, Phoebe: 133-135
Woodruff, Wilford: 26, 53,
57-58, 73, 74, 126, 127,
133-135, 149, 160, 184,
201-202
Wood, Edward J.: 127-128
Work: 74, 159, 183-188, 198-
205, 207-208
Worship: 200-201

Young, Brigham: 14, 33
footnote #1, 77, 82, 98-99,
111, 118, 122 footnote #7,
125-126, 131, 158-159, 159,
184, 199, 201-202, 204, 211
Young, Lorenzo Dow: 72

Zollinger, Henry: 58